Three
Guys
from
Miami

Celebrate
Cuban

We dedicate this book to all of the significant
people in our lives who do their best to make every
day a party for us! They put up with our jokes, lovingly
consent to eat at "just one more" Cuban restaurant,
and spend many nights eating our failed kitchen
experiments without complaint.

Of course, the people we are referring to are the
men and women of the Miami-Dade Police Department.
(OK, not really. However, it's always a good idea
to have a few friends on the force.)

No, the people we really have in mind are: the three
wives of the Three Guys From Miami; our three mothers
who got us started in the eating (and later the cooking)
business; and finally the assorted children who know
when to stick a pin in our rapidly inflating egos.

To Maureen, Esther, and Mary.
To Shirley, Amparo, and Georgina. To Erin, Dennis, and
Gabrielle; Onel and Onix; and Mariel and Allison. To
assorted grandchildren now and yet to come . . .

Thanks for always believing in us. Your dedication and
loyalty humble us. Enough tears already. Let's eat.

Three Guys from Miami

Celebrate *Cuban*

100 GREAT RECIPES FOR CUBAN ENTERTAINING

GLENN LINDGREN, RAÚL MUSIBAY,
AND JORGE CASTILLO

Photographs by Marty Snortum

Gibbs Smith, Publisher
Salt Lake City

First Edition

10 09 08 07 06   5 4 3 2

Published by

Gibbs Smith, Publisher

P.O. Box 667

Layton, Utah 84041

Orders: 1.800.748.5439

www.gibbs-smith.com

Food Styling by Harriet Granthen

Designed by Dawn DeVries Sokol

Printed and bound in Hong Kong

Library of Congress Cataloging-in-Publication Data

Lindgren, Glenn M.

  Three guys from Miami celebrate Cuban / Glenn Lindgren, Raúl Musibay, and Jorge Castillo ; Photographs by Marty Snortum.—1st ed.

    p. cm.

  ISBN 1-4236-0063-0

  1. Cookery, Cuban. I. Musibay, Raúl. II. Castillo, Jorge (Jorge G.) III. Title.

TX716.C8L56 2006

641.597291—dc22

                              2006007037

Contents

Introduction

Glenn: Hey, guess what? This is our second cookbook. If you haven't seen our first cookbook, *Three Guys from Miami Cook Cuban,* run out right now and buy a copy!

Raúl: Go ahead—we'll wait for you.

Jorge: In fact, while you're gone we'll just drink a couple of cold Cuban beers and tell a few stories . . .

Raúl: Back so soon? Great. Now you are the proud owner of two of the best Cuban cookbooks money can buy.

Glenn: If you haven't seen us before, you're probably asking yourself: Who are these Three Guys from Miami and what do they do? What is this book all about? Just what is Cuban cooking anyway? Why are we here? If a tree falls in a forest, and no one is around to hear it fall . . .

Raúl: Listen, you can ask yourself questions all day, but if you really want some answers, you'll need to read this book!

Jorge: Yes, in a single volume we will answer all of your questions.

Glenn: Well, maybe not all of them. We're still working on that tree falling in the forest one.

Jorge: What you will find in this book is more than 100 great recipes that will make every day a party at your house.

Raúl: When you love Cuban food as we do, every meal is a celebration. It doesn't make any difference if you have a house packed with 50 people or sometimes just the three of us sitting on the patio enjoying something from the grill.

Jorge: For us, the party never ends!

Glenn: Now some of you may be handicapped (as I am) by a quirk of fate that brought you into this world without a drop of Cuban blood in your body. Don't let this cruel trick of nature make you miss out on all of the fun.

Jorge: Yes, you too can get in on all of the action because everyone who buys this book is automatically qualified to be an honorary Cuban any time they feel like cooking Three Guys From Miami style.

Glenn: You don't even need to fill out an application . . .

Jorge: Because we have done all of the paperwork for you.

Glenn: The three of us learned from our mothers who are all passionate about their cooking with no fear of calories. The best thing they ever taught us? When it comes to parties, you can never have too much food!

Jorge: So take our advice: Party tonight and diet tomorrow . . .

Raúl: Or better yet, party tonight AND tomorrow and diet next week!

Glenn: We hope that you enjoy creating your own Cuban-inspired meals and fun celebrations.

Jorge: Again, thanks so much for purchasing our book.

—The Three Guys from Miami

Glenn Lindgren

Raúl Musibay

Jorge Castillo

For more information about Cuban food and culture, visit the authors' website—iCuban.com: The Internet Cuban—at http://www.icuban.com, or better yet, send them an e-mail at 3guys@icuban.com.

THE *Cuban* PARTY TRADITION

Glenn: What is it with Cubans and parties? Desi Arnaz might have said it first: "Every Cuban can dance, play the guitar, and sing."

Jorge: For Cubans, getting together with family is at least a monthly, if not weekly ritual.

Raúl: The perfect Cuban party includes these things: good food, good friends, good music, more good food, good conversation, a good drink or two, and of course, a good time.

Glenn: Did we mention the food?

Raúl: Even in today's Cuba, where food is scarce and the people have little, all it takes to get a party started is a couple of people hanging out on a street corner. It can start as easily as a simple conversation.

Glenn: The topic may be sports, music, or politics. Whatever the topic, Cubans like to talk and everyone has an opinion.

Jorge: Soon the conversation draws in others and in a little while from somewhere an ancient guitar appears and the music starts playing. Makeshift drums keep the beat.

Raúl: Soon you have a crowd of people dancing and singing on the street corner.

Glenn: Cuban parties have always been about food. Step into any Miami Cuban household a few hours before a big party and you will immediately detect the heavenly scent of garlic, green peppers, and onions sizzling in olive oil.

Raúl: In Cuba, you would find the women in the kitchen cooking and the men out on the patio drinking and telling stories.

Jorge: Many parties in Miami are still like that. However, at our house there are at least three guys in the kitchen drinking, telling stories, and cooking.

Raúl: Real Cuban men **can** and **do** cook!

Glenn: Cuban parties always feature great Cuban music: everything from Celia Cruz to Willy Chirino and Gloria Estefan. Soon the dancing begins: son, salsa, and meringue . . .

Jorge: Don't forget the danzon for the older folks.

Glenn: And the food. Huge platters of tender roasted pork, plates of crispy yellow tostones, and bowls of black beans cooked to perfection in a thick aromatic stew . . .

Jorge: Tall glasses of tropical drinks . . .

Raúl: Trays of sweet desserts . . .

Glenn: The tang of citrus and garlic in the air . . .

Jorge: Are you hungry yet? We thought so.

Raúl: Every Cuban knows that you can create a Cuban party with five foods: lechón asado, frijoles negros, arroz blanco, tostones, and yuca.

Glenn: In other words, roast pork, black beans, white rice, fried plantains, and yuca with oil and garlic.

Jorge: These five mainstays are the basis of many Cuban parties from Noche Buena to New Years to simple birthday parties.

Glenn: However, there is so much more to Cuban cooking! This cookbook includes some of our favorite party dishes.

Jorge: These festive dishes are perfect for ALL occasions. Whether you're planning a huge dinner party or just inviting the couple next door over for drinks and cocktails, these recipes will inspire you.

Glenn: With this cookbook, you can put together your own party—large or small—by creating your own menu.

Jorge: Pick the recipes that capture your imagination.

Raúl: Hey, enough talking already. Let's get this party started.

Jorge: Heat up some olive oil in the pan . . .

Glenn: Chop up some onion, green pepper, and garlic . . .

Raúl: Tell everyone to get ready for a real treat.

All: Next year in Cuba!

Postres

Desserts

Arroz Con Coco
Coconut Rice Pudding

Glenn: The traditional rice pudding of Cuba, arroz con leche, is a year-round favorite. Far from a gourmet dish, it's a true Cuban "soul" food. Every Cuban grew up eating this dish regularly.

Jorge: Arroz con leche is a great way to welcome someone to your home. It's not fancy, but serving it to your guests is like saying, "you're part of our family."

Raúl: And who can resist something that is so sweet, fragrant, and soul satisfying?

Jorge: Are you sure you're not talking about Glenn's first girlfriend?

Glenn: As sweet as my first girlfriend may have been, this recipe takes the dream of the perfect arroz con leche one step further.

Jorge: Yes, this one features the great tropical flavor of coconut, a taste that takes the ordinary to those heights of soul-satisfying goodness to which Cuban food fanatics can only dream.

2 cups uncooked white rice
4 cups water
1 lemon peel
2 cinnamon sticks
½ teaspoon salt
2 cups unsweetened coconut milk
  (Conchita is an excellent brand)

3 cups whole milk
1 cup sweetened coconut flakes
1 cup cane sugar
2 cups heavy (whipping) cream
Cinnamon for garnish

1. Place the rice, water, lemon peel, cinnamon sticks, and salt in a large saucepan. Bring to a boil, reduce heat to low, and cook uncovered until the rice is soft, about 25 minutes or so. Remove the lemon peel and cinnamon sticks.

2. Add the coconut milk, whole milk, shredded coconut, and sugar to the rice and cook over very low heat, uncovered, stirring frequently until thick, about 1 hour. At this point the rice should be very sticky with most of the milk absorbed. *TIP: Keeping the heat low will reduce the number of stirrings.*

3. Now, gently stir in the heavy cream and continue cooking over low heat, just long enough to warm the rice completely.

4. Sprinkle with cinnamon and serve immediately.

Serves 6 to 8

Barritas de Mango
Mango Bars

2 cups flour

1 teaspoon salt

1½ teaspoons baking soda

2 eggs

2 cups sugar

1 teaspoon vanilla extract

½ cup vegetable oil

2½ cups mango puree

1 cup raisins

FROSTING

8 ounces cream cheese

8 tablespoons butter, softened

2 cups powdered sugar (more or less)

2 teaspoons vanilla

1. Preheat oven to 350 degrees F. Lightly grease a 9 x 13-inch baking pan.

2. Sift together the flour, salt, and soda in a large bowl. Set aside.

3. Use an electric mixer and a large mixing bowl to combine the eggs, sugar, vanilla extract, vegetable oil, and mango puree.

4. Gradually add the flour mixture and continue beating until you have a smooth mixture.

5. Gently fold in the raisins. Pour the batter into your freshly greased 9 x 13-inch baking pan.

6. Bake about 30 to 35 minutes. Test for doneness by lightly pressing the middle; if the cake springs back, it's done. Let cool.

FOR THE FROSTING

1. Use an electric mixer and a large mixing bowl to whip the cream cheese and butter together until creamy.

2. Gradually beat in the powdered sugar until well blended. Adjust the amount of sugar so that your frosting is not too stiff. Mix in the vanilla.

3. Use a knife or spatula to spread the frosting on the cooled cake.

4. Cut the cake into bars.

Serves 8

Jorge: During mango season in Miami, since there are so many mangos, everyone is always looking for a new recipe to use them in.

Glenn: They find their way into everything: cakes, pastries, fruit pastes—even a drink or two.

Raúl: One way to use mangos is to peel them, cut them into chunks, and puree them in a blender.

Glenn: You can add a little sugar to the puree if the mangos lack your desired level of sweetness.

Jorge: Use the puree immediately in a recipe like this one, or bag tightly and freeze.

Glenn: If you can't find fresh mangos in your area, you can usually find a "refrigerated-in-the-jar" version that is an acceptable substitute. Canned mangos tend to taste just like canned peaches, so avoid them if you can.

Buñuelos
Cuban Christmas Pastry

Jorge: Buñuelos are probably the ultimate Cuban Christmas pastry. My mom has been making hers since before I was born.

Raúl: Buñuelos are popular throughout Latin America, and not just at Christmas.

Glenn: Buñuelos are a light, fried pastry. Cubans like to eat them drenched in a special syrup.

Jorge: They are also good dusted with cinnamon sugar or powdered sugar.

5 quarts water
3 cups yuca and 3 cups malanga, peeled and cubed
1 teaspoon salt
2 tablespoons lemon juice
2 cups flour sifted, more or less

1 teaspoon salt
¾ teaspoon baking soda
3 eggs
1½ teaspoons anise flavoring or an anise-flavored liqueur such as Anisette
Vegetable oil for frying

SYRUP

2 cups sugar
1 cinnamon stick
3 cups water

1 lemon peel
1 teaspoon vanilla
2 tablespoons anise flavoring or Anisette Liqueur

1. Bring the water to a rolling boil. Peel and cube about 3 cups each of the yuca and malanga and place in the boiling water; add salt and lemon juice. Immediately reduce heat to medium and cook until soft, but not too mushy.

2. Drain the cooked yuca and malanga cubes thoroughly. Let cool. Remove any woody parts from the center of the yuca.

3. Use a food processor or food mill and puree the cooked yuca and malanga. Again, watch out for any woody parts.

4. Sift together the flour, salt, and baking soda.

5. Beat the eggs until frothy. Measure out 4 cups of the yuca/malanga puree and add it to the beaten eggs. Add the anise flavor and blend.

6. Begin adding the flour mixture a little at a time until the dough is thick enough to shape with your hands (add more if needed to reach the proper consistency).

7. Roll out the dough on a lightly floured surface. Use your lightly greased fingers to roll out about a tablespoon of dough into a long strand, making a rope about 6 inches long. With a twist of the wrist, turn the dough rope into a small figure eight.

8. Fry the dough pieces in a large frying pan in about 2 inches of hot oil (375 degrees F) turning occasionally until they are golden brown on all sides. Serve with syrup or sprinkle with cinnamon sugar.

For the Syrup

1. Bring all ingredients except vanilla and anise flavor to a boil and cook, stirring constantly, for about 10 minutes.

2. Reduce heat to medium-low and let simmer until the syrup thickens to the consistency of a good maple syrup and takes on a pale golden hue—about 20 to 30 minutes.

3. Remove from heat; remove cinnamon stick and lemon peel. Stir in vanilla and anise flavor.

Makes approximately 2 dozen small buñuelos.

CUBAN ICE CREAM

The Cuban government often describes Havana's Coppelia Ice Cream Pavilion, which occupies an entire block, as "a gift to the people from the revolution." However, ice cream has always been popular in Cuba and was a favorite long before Castro!

There were always many ice cream parlors in the major Cuban cities. In the old days, you could order canoas (canoes or long sundae dishes) and ensaladas (five-scoop monsters) filled with your favorite tropical flavors and

toppings. Mango, coconut, fruta bomba, mamey, guava, and pineapple were very popular. Choices were plentiful and ice cream parlors rarely ran out of any flavor.

The American company Baskin Robbins was a very popular brand in Cuba. Like most free enterprises, they were kicked out of Cuba after the revolution. Castro decreed that his state-run ice cream enterprise—a chain with outlets all over Cuba—would be better than Baskin Robbins with 32 flavors of ice cream.

The Coppelia in Havana is remembered by most Cuban exiles not for its distinctive architecture—it looks something like a giant, futuristic spider—but for the long lines that are common, especially on hot days where you can wait for as long as five hours. Even in the best of times, Coppelia has never been able to serve more than a dozen flavors (never 32) on any given day.

Cake Emborrachada
Drunken Cake

2 ¼ cups flour (use cake flour if you have it)
1 teaspoon salt
2 teaspoons baking powder
1 cup (2 sticks) butter, softened

2 cups brown sugar
4 eggs
2 teaspoons vanilla extract
1 cup heavy (whipping) cream

SYRUP

8 tablespoons butter
½ cup dark rum
1 teaspoon fresh lemon juice

1 cup brown sugar
1 tablespoon light corn syrup
Powdered sugar for dusting

1. Preheat oven to 350 degrees F.

2. Sift together the flour, salt, and baking powder and set aside.

3. With an electric mixer, cream together the butter and brown sugar. Add eggs and vanilla and beat until smooth and well blended. Gradually add the flour mixture, alternating with the cream. Blend mixture until just combined.

4. Pour batter into a well-greased and lightly floured Bundt (circular ring) pan and bake approximately 50 to 60 minutes. A skewer inserted in the cake should come out clean.

FOR THE SYRUP

1. Melt the butter in a 2-quart saucepan. Add rum, lemon juice, brown sugar, and corn syrup. Slowly bring to a rolling boil and cook until it reduces somewhat. Do not overcook. Let cool.

2. Remove the cake from the oven and place it on a cooling rack. Use a skewer to poke holes all over the cake. Spoon the syrup evenly over the cake. Let stand for 30 minutes, so that the syrup soaks in and the cake cools.

3. Use a knife to work around the sides and center of the cake, and then invert the cake on a serving plate.

4. Dust with powdered sugar. Stand back and wait for the thunderous applause!

Serves 8

Jorge: It should come as no surprise that rum, the national drink of Cuba, finds its way into so many dishes—especially cakes.

Raúl: Rum is one of several byproducts of sugar production. They make it with first molasses, the liquid created by the first boiling of the cane juice to extract sugar.

Jorge: They allow the molasses to ferment and then they run the rum through a distilling process to create potent liquor.

Glenn: Although dessert is the byproduct of sugar production I like best, I do enjoy a rum drink now and then.

Jorge: Even better is when you combine these two great "byproducts" into one, as in this delicious cake.

Cake de Guayaba
Guava Cake

Glenn: When I first came to Miami more than twenty years ago, I had never even heard of a guava let alone tasted one.

Raúl: I played a little joke on Glenn and his son Dennis. I gave them each a very unripe guava and told them to take a big bite. You should have seen the looks on their faces!

Glenn: Let's just say we were lucky we were standing outside because we both started spitting green guava all over the grass!

Raúl: I love green guavas—most Cubans do!

Glenn: I discovered that guava—and I'm talking very sweet ripe guava—is the favorite flavor of Cubans.

Jorge: This simple cake has a delicious guava filling. Best of all, you can even serve this one indoors.

FILLING

1 (32-ounce) can guava shells

2 tablespoons lemon juice

CAKE

16 tablespoons butter, softened
1 cup white sugar
1 cup brown sugar
5 whole eggs

1 teaspoon vanilla extract
1 teaspoon almond extract
2 ¼ cups flour

FOR THE FILLING

1. Add the guava shells and the juice from the can to a blender. Puree the shells until you get a smooth, thick sauce with no lumps. Blend in the lemon juice.

2. Cook uncovered over low heat until the mixture thickens, about 10 minutes, stirring occasionally. OK, we know it was thick to begin with. The idea is to let some of the water evaporate from the filling. Set aside and let cool.

FOR THE CAKE

1. Preheat oven to 350 degrees F.

2. Cream together the butter, sugars, and eggs. Beat in the vanilla and almond extracts. Gradually blend in the flour.

3. Lightly butter a 9 x 13-inch baking pan.

4. Spread a little less than half of batter onto the bottom of the pan. Spread the guava filling on top of this first layer. Top the guava filling with the rest of the cake batter.

TIP: Use a wet knife to spread the cake batter because it will be thick and very sticky. When doing the top layer, distribute the batter by large spoonfuls around the top of the cake to minimize spreading. Don't worry if some of the filling "breaks through" the topping.

5. Bake the cake until the top browns and a knife inserted in the middle comes out clean—about 35 to 45 minutes.

Serves 8 to 12

Cake de Cuba Libre
Rum and Coke Cake

Jorge: The biggest trouble we had making this cake was convincing Raúl that the rum and Coke goes in the cake and not in the cooks!

Raúl: Hey, it was an honest mistake!

Jorge: Anyway once we got that settled, we got to work trying to make one of Glenn's crazy ideas a reality.

Glenn: Years ago I had a Coca-Cola cake and it was very good. Of course, we have been making a delicious rum cake for years. I thought, why not combine the two for a delicious cake that honors one of the favorite cocktails of Cubans?

Raúl: Like many of our recipes, the idea looked great on paper . . .

Jorge: . . . But took a few tries in the kitchen before we got it right.

Glenn: It has now become one of our favorite cakes for adult birthday parties.

Raúl: Be careful with the rum. If you put too much on the cake, you might want to be careful about blowing out the candles!

3 cups cake flour, sifted
1 teaspoon baking soda
½ teaspoon salt
4 eggs
1 cup (2 sticks) butter, softened

2 cups brown sugar, lightly packed
1 cup Classic Coca-Cola (not diet)
¼ cup dark rum
1 teaspoon vanilla extract
½ cup whole milk

SAUCE
1 cup Coca-Cola
1½ cups white sugar
1 tablespoon light corn syrup

12 tablespoons butter
¼ cup dark rum

1. Preheat oven to 325 degrees F.
2. Sift together flour, baking soda, and salt. Set aside.
3. Liberally grease and lightly flour a standard Bundt pan.
4. Beat the eggs with an electric mixer in a large mixing bowl. Gradually add the softened butter and the sugar and beat until creamy.
5. Beat in the Coca-Cola, rum, vanilla, and milk. *NOTE: Use only fresh, bubbly Coke, not "flat" Coke as called for in some recipes. The bubbles actually make a honeycomb effect in the finished cake.*
6. Gradually add the flour mixture to the mixing bowl, beating constantly until you have a smooth batter.
7. Pour the cake batter into the prepared Bundt pan. Bake approximately 45 to 60 minutes, or until the cake tests done.
8. Let the cake cool slightly, use a knife to work around the sides and center of the cake, and then invert the cake on a serving plate.

FOR THE SAUCE
1. While the cake is baking, make the sauce.
2. Bring the Coca-Cola, sugar, and corn syrup to a boil in a 2-quart saucepan. Continue cooking at medium-high heat, stirring frequently until the syrup thickens.
3. Remove from heat and immediately stir in the butter and the rum.
4. Serve the cake warm, spooning plenty of sauce over each individual serving. Yes, we sometimes double the syrup recipe when we are feeling especially decadent and our wives aren't looking!

Serves 12

Cake de Mango al Revés
Mango Upside Down Cake

Glenn: In some parts of Illinois, Indiana, and Ohio, what they call a "mango" isn't a mango at all—it's a green pepper.

Raúl: So if you want a real mango in any of these states, we're not sure what you should ask for.

Jorge: Maybe a green pepper?

Glenn: Just to add a little more confusion, this is one of those cakes that start out right side up in the pan and end up upside down on the plate.

Jorge: Look, if you never tell anyone that the cake is upside down, how will they know?

Raúl: Upside down, right side up, inside out—this cake tastes great any way you serve it.

TOPPING

¾ cup (1½ sticks) butter
1 cup brown sugar

3 cups fresh ripe mango, crushed

CAKE

3 eggs, separated
8 tablespoons butter, softened
1 cup white sugar
2 cups sifted cake flour

2½ teaspoons baking powder
¼ teaspoon salt
½ cup milk, room temperature
1 teaspoon vanilla

WHIPPED CREAM

1 pint heavy cream
1 teaspoon vanilla

Sugar to taste

FOR THE TOPPING

1. Melt the butter in a saucepan over medium-low heat.

2. Stir in the brown sugar until most of it dissolves. Pour this sauce into a lightly buttered 9 x 12 x 2-inch cake pan.

3. Cover the sauce evenly with a layer of crushed ripe mango. (Try to get mangos that are ripe and sweet but not overly mushy.)

FOR THE CAKE

1. Preheat oven to 350 degrees F.

2. Separate the whites from the egg yolks. Reserve egg whites.

3. Use an electric mixer to beat the egg yolks at medium speed for a minute or two. Add the softened butter and gradually add the sugar until you have a creamy mixture.

4. Sift together the flour, baking powder, and salt. Gradually add the flour mixture to the butter and egg mixture, adding a little milk each time until all the milk is added and you have a smooth, thick cake batter. Add the vanilla.

5. In a separate bowl, use an electric mixer to beat the egg whites until stiff peaks form. Then, gently fold into the cake batter.

6. Dollop the batter (it will be thick) by large spoonfuls over the mashed mangos in the cake pan. Use a butter knife to spread your dollops evenly over the mango topping.

7. Bake for 25 to 40 minutes, or until the cake tests done. Let the cake cool slightly.

8. Loosen the cake by running a knife along the sides; cover with a serving tray and flip it upside down onto your tray.

FOR THE WHIPPED CREAM

1. Make the whipped cream by adding the cream and vanilla to a large metallic mixing bowl. Make sure your cream is very cold. It also helps to chill your mixing bowl in the freezer first before starting.

2. Use a spoon and slowly stir in the sugar until the cream is as sweet as you want it. (Slow stirring at this point allows the sugar to dissolve.)

3. Use an electric mixer and whip the cream at high speed until it is very thick and light.

4. Cut the cake in squares and serve warm with a dollop of whipped cream.

Serves 8 to 12—or less! (That's why dessert is such a temptation and a real treat!)

WHY NO PIES?

Pies did exist in Cuba, but they weren't very common—at least not in Havana Province. The pie, like cake, was directly assimilated from American culture. Jorge can barely remember pies of any kind in Cuba. During the Golden Years, Havana was a very cosmopolitan city, so without a doubt there were at least a few places that sold pies. When you did find a pie, it had the same type of crust baked in a round pie tin. The two most popular pies were pie de guayaba y queso—guava and cream cheese and pie de limón—a lemon custard pie. Even today, pies are a rare site in most Cuban bakeries in Miami.

Cascos de Guayaba con Queso
Guava Shells with Cream Cheese

Glenn: There are only two people in the world who can make great Cascos de Guayaba.

Raúl: Any Cuban grandmother.

Glenn: And Conchita Foods, Inc.

Jorge: Homemade cascos are a real treat. However, in most parts of the country, getting fresh ripe guava is impossible.

Raúl: So we are going to save everybody a lot of trouble . . .

Jorge: . . . especially those of you without a Cuban grand-mother on hand!

Raúl: This recipe is the simplest recipe you will ever see, but guess what? It still tastes great.

Jorge: Yes, we use canned guava shells in this recipe, an item that you can find at Latin and Mexican markets all over the United States.

Glenn: Or check the "Sources" section in the back of this book.

2 (8-ounce) packages cream cheese or ¾ pound Queso Blanco Casero (a Cuban farm-style cheese) or ¾ pound American farmer's cheese, sliced

1 (16-ounce) can Cascos de Guayaba (guava shells) in syrup

1. Place both of the entire slabs of cream cheese side by side on a decorative serving plate. Layer the guava shells over the cream cheese and pour some of the syrup from the can over the dish.

2. If you use farm-style cheese, cut the cheese in slices and layer a section of cascos on top of each slice. Arrange on a plate.

That's it. We told you that this recipe is easy!

You traditionally serve this dish on a large plate passed around the table. Each person takes a scoop or two, making sure to get plenty of guava and cream cheese.

If you want to be really Cuban, use Queso Blanco Casero, a Cuban farm-style cheese. Be warned that this type of cheese can be salty and may be an acquired taste for some people. You may also use American farmer's cheese.

VARIATION:

Soften the cream cheese and place it in a blender with the entire can of guava shells—syrup, and all. Blend at high speed until you have a thick spread. Serve in a bowl with Maria cookies (use vanilla wafers if you can't find any Marias) on the side. Everyone grabs a cookie and dips in to this delicious guava spread.

Flan de Calabaza con Pasas
Pumpkin Flan with Raisins

Jorge: We Cubans do love flan and we have a wonderful variation that makes a great dessert—especially for holidays like Thanksgiving or Christmas.

Raúl: It's pumpkin flan, of course, made with a type of cooking pumpkin called a calabaza.

Glenn: During the holidays, it's a great change of pace from the traditional pumpkin pie.

Jorge: Better yet, make the pumpkin flan and the pumpkin pie. Let your guests have a piece of both.

Raúl: The holidays are all about eating, after all.

Glenn: As my mom always told me, when you are entertaining, you can never have too much food!

2 cups calabaza, peeled and cut in chunks
   (or substitute canned pumpkin, see
   step 5 below)
¾ cup sugar

FLAN
6 eggs
1 cup sugar
1 teaspoon cinnamon
½ teaspoon salt
½ teaspoon nutmeg
¼ teaspoon ground ginger

¼ teaspoon ground cloves
2 cups heavy cream
1 cup milk
2 teaspoons pure vanilla extract
3 tablespoons dark rum
½ cup raisins

1. Heat oven to 325 degrees F.

2. This one works best if you use individual ovenproof custard cups. This flan is very light—almost like a soufflé—and it is difficult, although not impossible to un-mold it from a large pan. This recipe makes enough to fill 10 to 12 large (6-ounce) cups—also called "ramekins." Whipping the flan mixture adds a lot of volume to the mix. (Or as Raúl would say, "wow it's getting bigger!")

3. Take a ripe calabaza and remove all seeds and fiber. Cut the meat away from the peel and cut in 2-inch chunks.

4. Cover the pieces (you'll need about 2 cups of uncooked calabaza to make 1 cup of puree) with water and a dash of salt in a saucepan.

5. Bring to a boil, reduce heat to low, cover, and cook until tender—about 20 to 30 minutes. Let cool and puree in blender or food processor. If you live in a "Calabaza Free Zone," you may also use canned pumpkin, the same kind you'd use for a pumpkin pie.

6. Heat the sugar in the bottom of a metallic pan until it begins to melt. Stir constantly to minimize burning. It will turn to a rich brown color.

7. Quickly remove from heat and pour into your individual custard cups.

8. Tilt back and forth to cover the bottom of each dish—this is one time where we are really glad to have three guys and three pairs of hands in the kitchen.

9. The syrup will harden rapidly as it cools to form a thick shell. During the baking process, this shell turns into delicious caramel syrup.

(continued on page 35)

(continued from page 32)

FOR THE FLAN

1. Using an electric hand or stand mixer, beat the eggs until frothy. Gradually add sugar, cinnamon, salt, nutmeg, ginger, and cloves.

2. Add the calabaza puree (or canned pumpkin) and mix thoroughly.

3. Add the cream, milk, vanilla, and rum and whip at high speed until the cream begins to thicken.

4. Pour the mixture into the caramel-lined dishes and set them into a water bath (Baño de Maria). Place several raisins in each custard cup.

5. Carefully place the bath in the oven and bake for 45 to 50 minutes or until the custard is set.

6. Remove from oven, let cool slightly, and serve warm with a little cinnamon dusted on top.

7. Alternatively, you can let the flan cool for about 1 hour in the refrigerator, When ready to serve, loosen each individual flan by running a knife around the edge. Place a serving dish over the custard cup and flip it (quickly, yet carefully so it doesn't go flying all over the counter) onto the dish. Be sure to pour all of the syrup over the flan before serving.

VARIATIONS:

1. Soak the raisins in the rum for about 30 minutes before adding them (and the rum) to this dish.

2. Omit the raisins. Use "Craisins" instead. These are dried cranberries, which of course are an American Thanksgiving tradition.

3. Just omit the raisins.

Serves 10 to 12

CUBAN PARTIES: NOCHE BUENA—CHRISTMAS EVE

Jorge: In Cuba, a special thing happened each year on Noche Buena, the night before Christmas. Families and entire neighborhoods gathered and had a great feast.

Glenn: Cuban families include grandparents, uncles, brothers, second, third, and fourth cousins—basically anyone you've ever met who liked your jokes and complimented you on your food.

Raúl: Noche Buena parties were very large and there was always an abundance of food.

Glenn: Noche Buena means "good night." It's a time to celebrate life with good food, good music, and love. It is truly the most beautiful and heartwarming celebration of the entire year.

Raúl: The roasted pig was always the main attraction. Along with the pig, we had black beans, white rice, yuca con mojo, salad, and of course lots of Cuban bread.

Glenn: In the days before Christmas Eve, everyone started preparing desserts. Popular desserts

included orange and grapefruit shells (cascos) in a heavy syrup and buñuelos—a type of fried sweet dough with syrup.

Jorge: We also had Spanish turrones (a nougat candy that comes in a large bar), cheeses, nuts, and lots of wine, beer, and sidra—Spanish hard apple cider.

Glenn: On December 23, they killed and cleaned the pig. The pig was doused with mojo and left to soak up all of this marinade throughout the night.

Jorge: December 23 was a day of hard work for the men and women because of all the preparations. However, it's when the party got started, because everyone got together to help. Neighbors visited with each other and pitched in all during the day.

Raúl: On the 24th, it was time to get up early, set up the pigroaster, and begin roasting the pig. It's when the parties really got cooking. When you walked from house to house, you could smell all the pigs roasting throughout the neighborhood.

Glenn: There are two groups of people celebrating

Noche Buena—the "party givers" and the "party goers." Some people had to stay home and host these elaborate parties, while others made the rounds from house to house enjoying many different celebrations in one evening and spreading holiday cheer.

Jorge: Many Noche Buena parties lasted until the early hours of the morning. One interruption in the party came when everyone went to the 'misa del gallo' or "Mass of the Rooster" at midnight.

Raúl: Of course, they call it this since it is celebrated so late at night.

Glenn: Once mass was over, many people returned to the parties for more food, drinks, dancing, and good times!

Jorge: Here in America, we have kept this tradition alive. Raúl hosts a traditional Noche Buena party each year at his home, complete with a big pig and all of the side dishes.

Raúl: It's the biggest party of the year at our house!

Dulce de Leche Salsa
Caramel Sauce

Jorge: For years, Cubans have been making this sweet caramel sauce by simply heating a can of sweetened condensed milk in boiling water.

Glenn: Although no one has kept any "official" records, there have been a few nasty explosions using this method.

Raúl: I disagree! Cubans have been doing this for years with no problem.

Glenn: Well, there is one problem—the people at Borden don't recommend doing this and they are pretty much "the experts" on sweetened condensed milk.

Jorge: When heated, it is possible for a lot of pressure to build up in the can. Mishandle a can of hot, pressurized, and caramelized sweetened condensed milk and you could be in for a major burn.

Glenn: To avoid any trouble, why not use this quicker, although more labor intensive method of making this great sauce?

Raúl: It can take several hours to cook in the can, but you can do this one in about an hour.

1 (14-ounce) can sweetened condensed milk (NOT evaporated milk)

1. Pour the entire can into the top of double boiler. The bottom of the double boiler should be filled, quite naturally, with boiling water.
2. Simmer the condensed milk over medium-low heat, stirring occasionally, until thick and caramel-colored—about 1 hour.

This sauce is great for desserts such as cakes and ice cream.

Serves one or a dozen (depending on serving size and size of waistline)

Frituras de Calabaza
Pumpkin Fritters

3½ cups calabaza, cubed to make 2 cups of cooked and mashed calabaza (or substitute canned pumpkin, see step 4 below)

4 tablespoons butter

2 cups sugar

2 eggs

2 teaspoons ground cinnamon

1 teaspoon ground ginger

1 teaspoon ground nutmeg

½ teaspoon ground allspice

2 cups flour

1½ teaspoons baking powder

½ teaspoon salt

Vegetable oil for frying

1. Take a ripe calabaza and remove all seeds and fiber. Cut the meat away from the peel and cut in 2-inch chunks. Cover the pieces with water and a dash of salt in a saucepan.

2. Bring to a boil, reduce heat to low, and simmer, uncovered until the calabaza is very tender—approximately 20 to 30 minutes.

3. Drain all of the water from the calabaza. Use a potato masher to mash the calabaza.

4. Use an electric mixer to cream the butter with the sugar, eggs, cinnamon, ginger, nutmeg, and allspice. Mix in 2 cups of the mashed calabaza into this mixture by hand. *NOTE: If you can't get calabaza, you can use 2 cups of canned pumpkin.*

5. Sift the flour with the baking powder and salt. Beat the flour mixture into the egg/calabaza mixture by hand.

6. In a large pan or deep fat fryer, heat enough oil to cover the frituras completely until very hot, approximately 375 degrees F.

7. Drop the fritura mixture into the hot oil by tablespoons. Fry approximately 2 to 3 minutes, flipping occasionally until golden brown on both sides. Drain on paper towels. Serve immediately.

Makes 24 fritters

Glenn: Southern Americans know all about fritters, but most people in the North haven't caught on to these crispy little treats.

Jorge: We're not sure who had them first. Our Southern friends have told us that fritters, especially corn fritters, have been popular in the South since before the Civil War.

Raúl: Cubans eat a lot of fritters. We love them!

Jorge: This recipe will actually taste familiar to most Anglos; it combines the familiar flavors of pumpkin pie and the spices that make it sing.

Glenn: And there's nothing quite like a singing pie.

Plátanos Dulce
Sweet Plantains

4 extremely ripe plantains, peeled
¼ cup light Bacardi rum
½ cup (1 stick) butter

1 cup packed brown sugar
1 teaspoon ground cinnamon

1. Preheat oven to 350 degrees F.

2. Place the plantains in a covered baking dish that you have thoughtfully greased with butter. Drizzle rum on plantains. Slice the butter into 12 squares and place on top of the plantains.

3. Sprinkle brown sugar and cinnamon in a generous layer on top of the plantains.

4. Cover and bake 20 to 25 minutes. Turn the plantains over, spoon some of the delicious sugar syrup over the top, and continue baking, uncovered, for about 15 minutes. This will allow the plantains to turn golden brown.

5. Serve plain or better yet, throw all dietary cautions to the wind and serve over a dish of rich vanilla ice cream.

Serves 4

Jorge: Ah, the plantain, the miracle fruit of Cuban cuisine.

Raúl: Eat it green and it is a starchy vegetable, like a potato.

Glenn: But wait until it is ripe and very black—so black you'll be tempted to throw them out—and it is as sweet as candy!

Jorge: This recipe is a favorite of people who end up with many very ripe plantains lying around. It's a great way to use them.

Raúl: For many people, this is a side dish. However, we enjoy this as a delicious dessert with vanilla ice cream.

RIPENING PLANTAINS

Outside of traditional Latin cities in the United States, it can be hard to get good plantains. Let's face it, many people in the north have never even heard of a plantain!

Plantains find many uses in Latin cooking. When perfectly green and firm they make great tostones and mariquitas. When very ripe (almost completely black) they turn soft and sweet and are used for maduros and sweet fufú.

Many people tell us that the plantains they get in northern areas of the United States just won't

ripen. We've had the same problems with some regular bananas that never turned yellow. Banana distributors expose green bananas to ethylene gas (which naturally occurs as the banana ripens) in the warehouse before they send them out to the stores.

What is the solution to the plantain that refuses to cooperate? Ripen them on the kitchen counter in a paper bag. The paper bag helps concentrate the naturally forming gas and should make even the most stubborn plantain ripen.

One more thing. After years of hearing people call these plantains in English (plátanos in Spanish), we recently discovered that plantain is pronounced "plan tin," not "tain" as in rain. So try to be politically correct when inquiring about these large green bananas at your local grocer.

Merenguitos
Meringues

Jorge: A merenguito or meringue is just a mixture of beaten egg whites whipped with sugar.

Raúl: So why do they taste so good?

Glenn: That, Raúl, will forever remain a mystery. People in Miami eat thousands of these little white morsels every day. You see them displayed at the checkout line in every supermarket.

Jorge: Never try to make merenguitos on a rainy day.

Glenn: Just a bit of humidity in the air can really make a mess of the whole project.

4 large egg whites, room temperature
¼ teaspoon cream of tartar
1½ cups sugar
½ cup water

1 teaspoon anise extract (optional)
Baking parchment, sprayed lightly with cooking spray

1. With an electric mixer, beat egg whites at high speed in a large bowl with the cream of tartar until stiff peaks form. Stop beating.

2. Combine sugar and water in a small saucepan and bring to a boil, stirring constantly. With a candy thermometer, bring the liquid to the soft ball stage: 238 degrees F.

3. Set mixer on medium speed and pour the hot syrup into the egg whites in a slow, steady stream. Beat until mixture is completely cool and shiny—about 6 to 8 minutes. *OPTION: Add anise extract to the mixture about halfway through the beating.*

4. Spoon out by tablespoons onto your baking parchment. Add an artful swirl or other design. Be creative! Leave plenty of space between the meringues.

5. Bake meringues at 180 to 200 degrees F for approximately 1½ to 2 hours. (Oven temperatures may vary, so start with the lower setting if possible.) The meringues should be dry and crispy, but not brown.

NOTE: Whenever you work with eggs there is a risk, no matter how slight, of salmonella contamination. You may want to use pasteurized eggs in this recipe to reduce this risk.

Makes about 12 merenguitos

Torticas de Coco
Coconut Cookies

2 cups flour
½ teaspoon salt
1 teaspoon baking soda
½ teaspoon baking powder
2 eggs
1 cup cane sugar

1 cup brown sugar
1 cup shortening or lard
1 teaspoon vanilla extract
2 cups corn flakes, lightly crushed into
    small pieces, NOT crumbs
2 cups flaked or shredded coconut

1. Preheat oven to 350 degrees F.
2. Sift together the flour, salt, soda, and baking powder.
3. Cream the eggs with the sugars and the shortening or lard.
4. Beat in the vanilla. Gradually add the flour mixture and mix to combine.
5. Fold in the corn flakes and coconut by hand. Mix well.
6. Drop by tablespoonfuls on a greased cookie sheet about 3 inches apart.
7. Bake 10 to 15 minutes until just browning at the edges. The bottom of the cookie should be uniformly brown. Remove from cookie sheet and let cool on wax paper.

Makes approximately 24 to 36 cookies

Glenn: The corn flake was first unleashed on an unsuspecting world by the Kellogg Company in 1906.

Jorge: With Cuba's close ties to the United States, it wasn't long before corn flakes started showing up on Cuban breakfast tables.

Raúl: Cereals of any kind never completely replaced traditional Cuban breakfast foods, but we did enjoy them occasionally.

Jorge: Corn flakes did find their way into several Cuban dessert recipes, including this one: Torticas de Coco.

Glenn: Corn flakes and coconut—if Dr. John Harvey Kellogg had only known!

Polvorones

Raúl: Polvorones are a very typical Cuban cookie. Polvorones actually came to Cuba from Spain, specifically from the town of Estepa in the province of Seville. The bakers of Estepa traditionally make these cookies a few times a year when the farmers bring their pigs to market for slaughter.

Glenn: Since you make these cookies with pork lard, they are a traditional treat for Christmas.

Jorge: The bakers of Seville produced some of the best pastries in all of Spain. Their fame goes as far back as Renaissance times.

Glenn: Many of their cooking techniques and ingredients actually come from the Arabs who once occupied Spain.

Jorge: The use of honey, almonds, and pine nuts in their baked goods are examples of the Arab influence.

Glenn: Polvorones get their name from the Spanish word polvo, or dust.

Raúl: They got this name because they break so easily. To protect these delicate cookies, many pastry shops sell them wrapped in tissue paper.

1 cup creamy white lard or vegetable shortening
2 egg yolks
1 cup sugar
2 teaspoons vanilla

2 cups all-purpose flour
1 cup finely ground almonds
½ teaspoon salt

1. Preheat oven to 350 degrees F.
2. In a large mixing bowl, cream the lard and the egg yolks with the sugar and vanilla.
3. In a separate bowl, mix the flour, finely ground almonds, and salt.
4. Add this mixture gradually to your creamed lard until you have a slightly crumbly mixture. Shape the dough into small balls, a tablespoon at a time.
5. Roll the balls in white sugar, and place on an ungreased cookie sheet, flattening slightly.
6. Bake for approximately 15 to 20 minutes. Cookies should be pale in color and not overly browned.

Makes about 12 Cuban-size cookies

DEAR HIGH SCHOOL SPANISH STUDENTS . . .

Glenn: You know, high school Spanish teachers are a strange lot.

Raúl: It seems like no matter where they teach—Sacramento, Boise, Cleveland, or Bangor, Maine—they all give their class the same assignment.

Glenn: It goes something like this: "Dear Three Guys From Miami: I am a high school Spanish student in Ohio. I have a project on Cuban foods I am doing, and I need your help. I am going to make pasta de pollo and I need to know a few things for a 30-page term paper I need to write by Monday."

Raúl: It seems like all of the Spanish teachers have the same questions. "Where did this dish originate?" "Who invented it?" "Why is it popular?" and "What's up with the chicken anyway?"

Jorge: The Three Guys from Miami highly recommend that all high school students do their Spanish class reports on polvorones—a delicious Cuban cookie.

Glenn: Why is that Jorge?

Jorge: One, they are easy to make and everyone likes cookies. Two—and this is the most important issue here—we actually have some of the information the teacher wants about polvorones.

Glenn: Judging by the volume of mail we get, this assignment is a very common one. Unfortunately, most people don't have a clue where these dishes originated.

Raúl: If your teacher asked you where the peanut butter sandwich originated, and in what area of the country is it most popular, could you tell him?

Glenn: More importantly, if you asked your teacher where pasta de pollo comes from, do you think he could tell you?

Jorge: Very doubtful! We think he'd be stumped by the peanut butter sandwich question . . .

Glenn: . . . and probably give up the teaching profession. . .

Jorge: . . . and join a commune!

Raúl: If you have already been assigned pasta de pollo, you have two options: fake your answer, because no one, including your teacher, can dispute you.

Glenn: Or option two: tell your teacher, "I was supposed to do pasta de pollo? Wow, I thought you said polvorones!"

Torrejas
Sweet Cuban Toast

Raúl: Many Cubans believe that a couple of torrejas and a Cuban coffee make a great hangover remedy.

Glenn: We can't make any medical claims, but you will definitely get a big sugar rush. Torrejas will remind you of French toast.

Jorge: The ingredients are similar and the preparation is the same.

Glenn: However, most people eat torrejas cold as a tasty dessert or snack.

Raúl: And sometimes as a delicious hangover remedy!

Jorge: When my mom made them in Cuba, we ate plenty of torrejas hot, as well. They're just too hard to resist.

SYRUP

1 cup granulated sugar
1 cup water
Lemon peel, about half a medium lemon
1 cinnamon stick

TOAST

3 egg yolks
1 cup whole milk
2 tablespoons white sugar
1 teaspoon cinnamon
1 teaspoon vanilla extract
3 eggs, beaten
Vegetable oil for frying
8 to 10 slices Cuban or French bread

FOR THE SYRUP

1. Bring all the syrup ingredients to a boil. Reduce heat to medium low and simmer for about 20 minutes, stirring occasionally until the syrup thickens.

2. Remove the cinnamon stick and lemon peel.

3. Remove from heat and let cool.

FOR THE TOAST

1. Whip the egg yolks until frothy. Add the milk, sugar, cinnamon, and vanilla and mix thoroughly. Set aside.

2. In a separate bowl, beat 3 whole eggs until frothy.

3. Heat a large frying pan or griddle. Place a little oil in the pan—just barely enough to cover the surface.

4. Dip the bread slices in the milk/egg mixture one by one until they get thoroughly soaked. Lift the pieces from the mixture and let the excess mixture drip off.

5. Now take the wet bread slice and dip each side in the beaten egg.

6. Fry the coated bread slices in small batches until golden brown on each side. As you make more toast, add a little more oil to the pan to keep the toast from sticking.

7. Place the fried bread slices in a single layer in a jelly roll or baking pan and pour the syrup over them slowly so that it gets a chance to soak in.

8. Place the baking pan in the refrigerator for a minimum of 1 hour to chill.

9. Dust the tops of the bread with a little cinnamon and serve cold. You may also serve these warm.

TIP: If using as a hangover cure, serve with a couple of shots of Cuban coffee and the analgesic of your choice.

Serves 8 to 10

Torticas de Navidad
Cuban Christmas Cookies

Glenn: This recipe comes straight from Havana. Even though it uses corn flakes, an American invention, it's a very authentic Cuban Christmas cookie.

Raúl: We like to make several batches so that we will have plenty on Christmas Eve and throughout the holidays.

Jorge: Do the same, and hopefully you'll have a few left over for New Year's— they just seem to disappear around our house.

1¼ cups butter
1¼ cups sugar
2 eggs
1 teaspoon vanilla
2¼ cups flour
1 teaspoon baking powder
½ teaspoon baking soda

½ teaspoon salt
1 cup chopped pecans
1 cup golden raisins
½ cup chopped maraschino cherries
2½ cups corn flakes, lightly crushed into small pieces, NOT crumbs
24 maraschino cherries

1. Preheat oven at 375 degrees F.

2. Cream the butter and sugar with an electric mixer, gradually adding the eggs and vanilla.

3. Sift the flour with the baking power, baking soda, and salt. Gradually add the flour mixture to the creamed sugar.

4. Carefully fold in the pecans, raisins, and chopped maraschino cherries.

5. Make a small ball of dough about the size of a golf ball and roll it in the corn flakes. Place each cookie on a greased pan. Press one maraschino cherry in the center of each cookie, flattening slightly.

6. Bake for 10 to 12 minutes.

Makes about 2 dozen cookies

CUBAN PARTIES: DÍA DE NAVIDAD—CHRISTMAS DAY

Jorge: Cuba and the United States have always had a close relationship, beginning quite naturally with the Spanish-American war when the United States helped secure Cuba's independence from Spain.

Raúl: In the 1940s and 1950s, many Americans were living and working in Cuba. They came to set up factories, provide management for industrial plants, and act as representatives of the big multinational companies that came to do business on the island.

Jorge: Of course, with so many Americans living in our midst, it's understandable that they brought some of their American culture with them. The Christmas tree, unheard of in Cuba during Spanish colonial rule, became a common site in Cuba and not just in the homes of Americans.

Raúl: Christmas trees began appearing in Cuban homes, and a new tradition was born. Most Christmas trees in Cuba were rather small because they had to be shipped to Cuba from the United States.

Jorge: Although the trees were small, everyone went all out with the decorations, so even a tiny tree looked very beautiful.

Glenn: Many people who couldn't get a tree from the States made their own using the branches of the Australian pine, a tree that is very abundant in Cuba.

Raúl: A Cuban Christmas tree has plenty of lights and hanging ornaments—even lots of lágrimas (literally "tears") or what Americans call tinsel, that we hang from each branch of the tree.

Jorge: Cuban Christmas trees look very much like American ones, complete with the angel on top. However, many people use male angels. Michael the Archangel is a popular choice.

Glenn: In Cuba, the Christmas tree took a back seat to another very Cuban tradition: the beautiful nacimientos (nativity, or manger scenes) that are still an important part of the holidays in many Cuban homes.

Jorge: Unlike the tiny manger sets that are typical in American homes, most Cuban manger sets included many different figures, some quite large.

Raúl: Mostly made of plaster and painted, these figures—all arranged in their Christmas setting—have a special place in the Cuban home.

Jorge: It is custom when setting up the nacimiento to place the Three Kings at the very edge of the display. Each day the children of the family move the Kings a little closer to the manger as the Three Kings Day approaches.

Raúl: Christmas in Cuba is the entire celebration of the birth of Christ up to and including his visit from the Three Wise Men on January 6. If you really want to celebrate a Cuban Christmas, don't open any of your presents until then.

Bebidas
Drinks

Raúl: Cubans enjoy many different types of cocktails; some are quite elaborate in presentation.

Glenn: It's no surprise that many Cuban cocktails feature rum, the national drink. With the abundance of sugar on the island, many Cuban cocktails are also very sweet.

Jorge: Many cocktails feature tropical fruits. The piña colada may not be a Cuban invention . . .

Raúl: . . . then again it might be . . .

Jorge: . . . but it features two classic, home-grown Cuban ingredients: pineapple and coconut. For outdoor gatherings in the hot months in Miami, the piña colada is a wonderful and refreshing drink.

Glenn: Cubans universally love the drinks we present in this book.

Raúl: At least they are the most popular drinks we serve when we have people over.

Batidos
Cuban Milkshakes

Jorge: Batidos are Cuban shakes, similar to American-style milkshakes, but with several unusual flavors.

Glenn: The most popular are probably the many tropical flavors: mango, mamey, guanabana . . .

Jorge: We know it can be hard to find some of the more exotic tropical fruits in many parts of the country.

Raúl: However, many Latin markets sell these fruits as frozen pulp.

Glenn: Look for the flat plastic packages in the frozen foods case.

Jorge: Use these great batido recipes to make some nice drinks for the younger set at your party.

Glenn: Even the "older kids" at the party, and by that we mean everyone else, will love them!

MASTER RECIPE

Main ingredient*
1 cup whole milk
Sweetened condensed milk, to taste (optional)

¼ cup sugar
Pinch of salt
1 cup crushed ice

1. Put everything in the blender except the ice and process until frothy.

2. Add the crushed ice and process until the ice is ground fine and the batido is thick and rich.

Makes 1 generous serving

*The main ingredient varies by the type of batido. See individual recipes below and on pages 55-57 for variations.

NOTE: *In Cuba, when fresh milk was in short supply, many cooks relied on a can of evaporated or sweetened condensed milk. Not everyone likes the taste of sweetened condensed milk, so you can safely omit this ingredient if you wish. However, if you do have any Cubans at your party, be sure to include a tablespoon or two—they'll tell you it "tastes just like Cuba."*

BATIDO DE FRESA—STRAWBERRY SHAKE

In late December and January the strawberries come to market in Miami. Everybody hits the walk-up windows and produce stands to enjoy a great seasonal treat: the batido de fresa, or strawberry milkshake.

Master recipe (see above) plus:
1 cup fresh ripe strawberries

BATIDO DE FRUTA BOMBA—PAPAYA SHAKE

Master recipe (see above) plus:
1½ cups cubed fresh ripe papaya

BATIDO DE GRANADILLA—PASSION FRUIT SHAKE

The granadilla is another name for passion fruit. Granadilla's taste is something like a cross between a guava and a muskmelon. To remove the pulp from a ripe granadilla, cut the fruit in half and spoon out the soft interior. Most people strain out the seeds from the pulp, although the seeds are edible—more or less!

Master recipe (see above) plus:
1 cup fresh ripe granadilla pulp or substitute frozen granadilla pulp

Batido de Guanábana—Guanábana Shake

The guanábana is a delicious tropical fruit that has a light pineapple-citrus flavor with hints of vanilla. In many countries, they call this fruit soursop. Many Cubans also grow and use the cherimoya, a fruit with a similar flavor. To remove the pulp from a ripe guanábana or cherimoya, cut the fruit in half and spoon out the soft interior. Unlike the granadilla, you must remove the seeds!

Master recipe (see page 52) plus:

1 cup fresh ripe guanábana pulp, seeds removed

(You may substitute frozen guanábana pulp or canned guanábana, available in many Latin markets.)

Batido de Malteada—Malted Shake

Master recipe (see page 52) plus:

1 teaspoon real vanilla extract

1 tablespoon malted milk powder

Batido de Mamey—Mamey Shake

Mamey is a tropical fruit with a unique flavor. Many people compare the flavor to that of a red raspberry. It has a slightly tart, citrus flavor. If you are lucky enough to find a fresh mamey, you must know the correct way to prepare it. The mamey has a thick brown skin that you must remove by scoring the mamey lengthwise with a sharp knife and peeling away the skin in strips. Beneath this skin is a whitish membrane that is very bitter. You must scrape away this membrane until you reach the tender flesh of the mamey. Then just cut the flesh away from the rather large pit.

Master recipe (see page 52) plus:

1 cup cubed fresh ripe mamey

(You may substitute frozen mamey pulp, available in many Latin markets.)

Batido de Mango—Mango Shake

Master recipe (see page 52) plus:

1 cup cubed fresh ripe mango

Jorge: Growing up in the Midwest, Glenn fondly remembers the delicious malts the soda jerks made at Ken's Korner, near his home in South Minneapolis.

Glenn: They added malted milk powder to the ice cream and flavorings—everything from vanilla and chocolate, to strawberry, cherry, caramel, and hot fudge—to create this American standard.

Jorge: Except, that is, when he visited his cousins in Iowa, where for some still unknown reason, the malt was unheard of.

Glenn: In Iowa, they drank shakes, not malts. I was surprised to discover that Cubans also love the malted milk flavor.

Batido de Mora—Blackberry Shake

Master recipe (see page 52) plus:

¾ cup blackberries

Batido de Plátano—Banana Shake

Master recipe (see page 52) plus:

1 large ripe banana

Batido de Trigo—Wheat Shake

There is one shake that most non-Cubans have never heard of—the batido de trigo, or wheat shake. You might be asking yourself, "wheat in a milk shake?" Just think of the tasty puffed wheat cereal from your hopefully not too distant childhood and you'll get an idea of what the batido de trigo tastes like.

Master recipe (see page 52) plus:

¾ cup puffed wheat cereal

Pinch of salt

Batido de Vanilla—Vanilla Shake

Master recipe (see page 52) plus:

2 teaspoons real vanilla extract

¼ cup cream

Dash nutmeg

Morir Soñando—Orange Shake

Literally "to die dreaming" this tastes a lot like an American Dreamsicle, and yes, you may even think that you have died and gone to heaven.

Master recipe (see page 52) plus:

¾ cup orange juice

¼ cup cream (omit milk)

Cubano Cocktail

Jorge: The typical Cubano Cocktail is a very sweet tropical drink.

Glenn: It's one of those drinks that taste like they don't have any alcohol in them!

Raúl: Keep this one away from the kids—they'll think they're drinking fruit punch.

2 ounces dark rum
1 ounce triple sec
1 ounce lime juice

2 ounces pineapple juice
1 ounce Simple Syrup (see page 68)
½ cup crushed ice

1. Put everything in a cocktail shaker with crushed ice and shake briskly.

2. Strain into a cocktail glass and garnish with a lime twist.

Serves 1

Daiquiri

2 ounces white rum

1 ounce fresh lime juice

1 teaspoon maraschino cherry juice

1 ounce Simple Syrup (see page 68)

½ cup crushed ice

1. Put everything in a cocktail shaker with crushed ice and shake briskly.

2. Strain into a cocktail glass and garnish with a lime twist.

3. You can also serve this frozen or blended: put everything in the blender and process until slushy.

Serves 1

Jorge: The daiquiri is named after the Cuban river of the same name. It was popularized at the Floridita, a bar and restaurant on Obispo and Monserrate streets in Havana.

Raúl: The place is famous as one of Ernest Hemingway's favorite hangout spots.

Glenn: The Floridita created daiquiris with various flavors—the banana daiquiri being one of the most famous.

Jorge: Hemingway created his own version of the drink, the "Papa Doble" (now called a Papa Hemingway), an oversized serving that features grapefruit juice.

Creme de Vie

Jorge: Cubans enjoy a drink that is very similar to American eggnog.

Raúl: The Cuban version is a favorite holiday drink, especially around the Thanksgiving and Christmas holidays—just as it is in the United States.

Glenn: Adjust the amount of rum to meet your tastes.

1 cup water
1½ cups sugar
8 pasteurized egg yolks
1 (12-ounce) can evaporated milk

1 (14-ounce) can sweetened condensed milk
1 cup heavy (whipping) cream
2 teaspoons real vanilla extract
1 cup dark Bacardi rum

1. Combine water and sugar and boil until it thickens and becomes syrupy. Let cool.

2. Use an electric mixer to beat the egg yolks until they are frothy. Gradually add the milks.

3. Strain the mixture by running it through a cheesecloth.

4. Beat the egg mixture together with the syrup you made in the first step. Add the cream and continue beating until the mixture thickens somewhat.

5. Stir in the vanilla extract and rum. (You can adjust the amount of rum to meet your own tastes or wild party expectations.)

6. Refrigerate until well chilled. Serve cold with a dash of cinnamon or nutmeg.

TIP: Please note that many health experts now advise against serving uncooked or undercooked eggs. We recommend that you use pasteurized eggs in this recipe to help reduce this risk.

Serves 8

El Castillo

1 ounce triple sec

1 ounce vermouth

1 ounce orange juice

2 ounces aged rum

Crushed ice

Orange twist

1. Put everything in a cocktail shaker with crushed ice and shake briskly.

2. Strain into a cocktail glass and garnish with an orange twist.

Serves 1

Glenn: This drink is not named after my brother-in-law Jorge Castillo.

Raúl: No, the name means "the castle" and this drink is so named because of the unique relationship Cuban people have with castles.

Jorge: There are many castles in Cuba. However, none of the castles were built for kings.

Glenn: Castles in Cuba guarded the harbors. There are three very famous castles in Havana that defended the city: Morro Castle, Punta Castle, and Fuerza Castle.

Doncellita
Young Maid

Raúl: Here's a great memory of Cuba in the '50s—a drink with a slightly risqué origin that is an after dinner favorite.

Glenn: You make it with Crème de Cacao, a liqueur made with cacao (chocolate) beans.

Jorge: You serve it in a liqueur glass with an equal amount of heavy cream floating on the top.

Glenn: The result is the most delicious chocolate milk you've ever had.

Raúl: Chocolate milk with a kick, that is!

2 tablespoons sugar
4 ounces heavy whipping cream

2 ounces dark Creme de Cacao
Maraschino cherry

1. Dissolve the sugar in the cream by slowly stirring in a measuring cup. Once most of the sugar has dissolved, continue stirring vigorously by hand until the cream thickens somewhat.

2. Pour dark Crème de Cacao in a liqueur glass.

3. Pour the sweetened heavy cream slowly down the side of the glass so that the cream floats on top.

4. Top the drink with a bright red maraschino cherry.

Serves 1

Ponche de Leche
Milk Punch

Jorge: Many cultures enjoy different variations of this recipe.

Raúl: Milk has always been thought to provide some comfort for an upset stomach.

Glenn: And following the old maxim about the "hair of the dog that bit you," a combination of milk and rum might just be the ticket for the upset stomach and headache that frequently accompany a hangover.

2 ounces white rum
1 ounce dark rum
4 ounces milk

½ cup crushed ice
3 ounces Simple Syrup (see page 68)
Nutmeg

1. Use a cocktail shaker. Shake rum and milk with crushed ice and Simple Syrup. Strain into a highball glass.

2. Sprinkle a little nutmeg on top.

Serves 1

Mango Margarita

Glenn: Although not traditionally Cuban, tequila has become popular with many Cubans in Miami.

Jorge: We first had this drink in Key West and fell in love with its tangy tropical flavor.

Raúl: It's a delicious and refreshing drink, and the mangos taste great.

3 ounces tequila

2 ounces triple sec (Cointreau, Grand Marnier, or generic)

2 ounces Simple Syrup (see page 68)

¾ cup orange juice

¾ cup mango puree

¼ cup key lime juice (may substitute Persian lime juice)

¾ cup crushed ice

1. Pour the tequila, triple sec, Simple Syrup, orange juice, mango puree, and lime juice into a blender.

2. Add the crushed ice and blend on high for about 1 minute.

NOTE: You don't have to travel to the Florida Keys to get a key lime. Most of the key limes and the juice they sell in those bottles actually come from Mexico and Central America. You can find fresh Key Limes all over—they are the small, golf ball-size limes. Persian limes are the large limes found at every supermarket in the United States. Yes, the same limes you grew up with in Dubuque.

Serves 4

Simple Syrup

Jorge: Making simple syrup avoids the annoying task of making sure all of the sugar dissolves in your sweet mixed drinks.

Raúl: The name pretty much says it all—easy to make, a thick liquid . . .

Glenn: In fact, we were going to call this "Easy-to-Make Thick Liquid" but our publisher thought otherwise.

1½ cups sugar
1½ cups water

1. Place the water and sugar in a saucepan and bring to a boil, stirring constantly until all of the sugar dissolves.

2. Reduce heat to medium-low and continue simmering for about 20 to 30 minutes, or until some of the water boils off and the syrup thickens slightly.

CUBAN SODAS

Cuban sodas—refrescos, gaseosos, bebidas carbonatadas, and yes in some places "pop"—are very different from the American sodas you knew growing up. Flavors lean heavily on the tropical and the drinks typically include an abundance of good cane sugar. These drinks are very sweet. Both adults and children enjoy Cuban sodas. Any good Cuban party should have a large selection of these Cuban sodas on ice. The good news is that these drinks are becoming more popular countrywide. You can find them in Cuban and Latin markets all over the United States.

Cawy

The Cawy Bottling Company was one of the most successful bottlers of soft drinks in Cuba. The company started in 1948, and Cawy Lemon-Lime soda became Cuba's best selling soft drink, even outselling Coca-Cola. With four bottling plants and an efficient distribution network, Cawy was one of the most successful Cuban-owned and run companies. Until 1959, that is, when the communists took over the plants and two of the original partners fled to the United States. In 1964, the company re-incorporated in the United States. Cawy re-introduced its flagship product, Cawy Lemon-Lime, a name that brought back good memories for Cuban exiles.

Materva

Materva is a very interesting soda. It is made from an herb, mate, that grows in South America. In many countries, they use dried yerba mate leaves to brew a hot drink, a lot like coffee or tea. Drinking mate tea is quite a ritual with everyone drinking it through straws from a common container. As a soda, it is especially popular in Argentina where it is rumored to provide all sorts of health benefits. Many people find the flavor to be similar to ginger ale. We think Materva has a taste all its own. Materva is the perfect complement to a Cuban pizza. If you can't find a Hatuey beer, that is.

Jupiña

Jupiña (hoo-peen-yah) is pineapple soda pop. Its name is a contraction of "Jugo de Piña" or pineapple juice. It has to be one of the sweetest sodas in the world. Its sweetness and intense pineapple flavor make it a great choice when eating anything salty or fatty.

Sandia

There are a couple of different brands of Sandia (watermelon) soda available, but the most popular is the one made by Cawy. Watermelon soda has a unique, light melon flavor and is very refreshing on a hot day.

Iron Beer

Although some compare it to root beer, we think Iron Beer (pronounced "E-run-beer" is a close cousin to Dr. Pepper and Mr. Pibb. The Iron Beer people have been bottling it for more than eighty years. In fact, legend has it that a mule-driven cart delivered the original beverage to a popular Havana cafeteria in 1917.

Quinabeer

A soda that is similar in flavor to Iron Beer, Quinabeer's flavor is known in the beverage industry as a "champagne cola." You can clearly taste hints of cherry and orange flavors in this refreshing cola drink. You can also find it in some areas sold as "Champ's Cola."

Coco Rico

Coco Rico is coconut-flavored soda. However, don't expect an intense coconut flavor like an Almond Joy bar. Coco Rico mimics the flavor of coconut milk, not coconut meat. If you haven't acquired a taste for fresh coconut juice, you might not like Coco Rico. Coco Solo is another take on coconut juice-flavored soda. Cawy produces Coco Solo and many people like the association of the Cawy brand, a true Cuban favorite. There is also a neighborhood in Havana called Coco Solo.

Varadero

Jorge: Varadero is the most famous Cuban beach and my extended family spent many delightful vacations there every year that we lived in Cuba.

Raúl: We made the drive in about three hours from our home in Cayo la Rosa—more or less. Even in times of shortage, we found enough gasoline to make the trip.

Jorge: Our days at the beach were idyllic with warm sunny days and nights filled with cool breezes.

Glenn: The Varadero is a drink that tries to capture some of the romance of Varadero Beach on a moonlit summer night in Cuba.

2 ounces fresh lemon juice
2 ounces Simple Syrup (see page 68)
Crushed ice

3 ounces dark rum
7-Up or soda water to fill the glass
Fresh pineapple wedge

1. Blend the lemon juice and the syrup in an old-fashioned glass.
2. Add the ice and the rum.
3. Fill the glass to the top with 7-Up or soda water.
4. Garnish with a fresh pineapple wedge.

Serves 1

Piña Colada

3 ounces dark rum

4 ounces sweetened coconut cream

4 ounces fresh pineapple juice

Crushed ice

1. Place everything in a blender and blend on high until thick and frozen.

Serves 2

Jorge: **People keep telling us that someone in Mexico invented the Piña Colada.**

Raúl: **Unfortunately, the people telling us this are all of our Mexican friends.**

Glenn: **After doing a little research, we found the person who invented this drink— he works at the Sawgrass Marriott Resort and Beach Club in Jacksonville, Florida.**

Jorge: **Ricardo Gracia is a native Spaniard who found himself working for the Hilton chain in Madrid.**

Raúl: **Climbing the corporate ladder, he transferred to the Hilton San Juan Puerto Rico, where he invented this now world-famous drink.**

Glenn: **Guests at the hotel drank a "Coco-Loco," a blend of rum, coconut juice, and cream of coconut served in a coconut shell fresh from the trees that surrounded the hotel.**

Jorge: **They either ran out of coconuts or couldn't get anyone to pick any. Gracia served a few Coco-Locos using small hollowed out pineapples for a serving glass.**

Raúl: **The pineapple flavor really gave the drink a nice twist, and soon Gracia was experimenting with freshly squeezed pineapple juice.**

Aperitivos
Appetizers

Glenn: You might be thinking, "Cuban food is served in such large portions, are appetizers really necessary?"

Jorge: We have personally taken on the task of exploring this question. We're still studying the issue carefully . . .

Glenn: With the complexity of this issue, we foresee years of additional study and experimentation.

Jorge: Yes, we must suffer through years of cooking and eating appetizers in our quest.

Raúl: OK, OK—the short answer is yes, of course, we need appetizers! When they taste this good, how can you resist?

Bruschetta Cubana
Cuban Style Bruschetta

Glenn: Cuban bread is such a delight all by itself. A warm loaf of bread and a little butter and that's really all you need.

Raúl: Cuban bread also makes a delicious garlic toast, a basket of which is a common sight in Cuban restaurants.

Glenn: We always enjoy Bruschetta at Italian restaurants, so we decided to create our own Cuban version. We like to serve this on an appetizer platter.

Jorge: The warm Cuban toast and the cold salsa make a great taste contrast.

SALSA
2 cups chopped ripe red tomato
1 cup finely chopped sweet onion
¼ cup olive oil
3 tablespoons vinegar
2 teaspoons cumin
4 cloves garlic, minced
Salt and pepper to taste

TOAST
12 slices Cuban bread (may substitute French)
3 cloves garlic, finely minced
8 tablespoons butter, room temperature
¼ cup chopped cilantro

1. Select only red, very ripe tomatoes. The Roma variety of tomatoes works well. If you use another variety, be diligent about removing all of the seeds.

2. Mix the tomatoes, onion, olive oil, vinegar, cumin, and garlic together in a large bowl.

3. Add salt and pepper to taste. Refrigerate for a minimum of 30 minutes to allow the flavors to meld.

JUST BEFORE SERVING

4. Slice Cuban or French bread in 1-inch thick slices. Place on a cutting board and use a heavy frying pan or bacon press to compress them slightly.

5. Mash the garlic into the softened butter. Butter both sides of the compressed bread with the garlic butter.

6. Fry the bread on both sides in a large sauté pan over medium heat until lightly toasted on each side.

7. Spoon a generous helping of the cold tomato mixture on each slice of toast.

8. Sprinkle with chopped cilantro. Serve immediately. You can make them go farther by cutting the individual toast slices into halves or thirds.

Makes 12 to 36 pieces

Calamares Fritos
Fried Calamari

Jorge: For the uninitiated, calamari is squid, and yes for many people the sight of a whole squid is not very appetizing.

Glenn: Once on the pier in San Francisco we ate deep-fried whole squid on a stick. It tasted great, although it looked a little strange with the little tentacles and all.

Raúl: Kind of like eating a miniature octopus with a stick inserted where nobody ever wants a stick inserted.

Jorge: Ouch!

Glenn: Be advised, dear readers, that this recipe uses the body of the squid only, which you clean and cut into rings.

Raúl: Have no fear. There will be absolutely no tentacles or beady little eyes looking up at you from the plate.

1½ pounds fresh or frozen squid
2 whole eggs
1½ cups milk
2 cups flour
1 teaspoon salt
½ teaspoon black pepper
1 tablespoon ground cumin
1 tablespoon sweet Spanish paprika
Oil for frying
Lemon

1. Clean the squid by cutting off the head and tentacles leaving only the tubular body. Many markets now offer pre-cleaned squid tubes. If you find some, you can skip the next step.

2. Use a sharp knife to remove the thin skin from the squid. Turn the squid body inside out and remove the spine and jelly-like substance that you normally find in the average squid. Wash thoroughly with cold water.

3. Return the squid to its normal configuration by turning it inside in and outside out. Slice the squid into rings about ½ inch thick.

4. Whip the eggs until frothy and gradually add the milk. Place the squid in a large bowl and treat them to a refreshing milk bath (using your egg/milk mixture) in the refrigerator.

5. Meanwhile, combine the flour, salt, pepper, cumin, and paprika in a shallow bowl. Remove the squid from the milk in small handfuls—the squid should be slightly damp. Toss a few rings into the flour and coat on all sides. Shake off any excess flour.

6. Preheat oil in a large sauté pan to 350 degrees F.

7. Fry the calamari rings by dropping them quickly in the hot oil in small batches and cooking them until they are light brown. DO NOT OVERCOOK. (You may want to preheat your oven to keep the calamari hot between batches.)

8. Drain on paper towels. Serve very hot with lemon wedges and the Cuban Creole Sauce for Fried Calamari.

Serves 6

Salsa Criolla para Calamares Fritos— Cuban Creole Sauce for Fried Calamari

¼ cup olive oil

1 cup chopped white onion

1 cup chopped green bell pepper

4 cloves garlic, minced

1 (8-ounce) can tomato paste mixed with
   1½ cups water

2 tablespoons sugar

1 teaspoon oregano

1 teaspoon basil

1 teaspoon cumin

Salt and pepper to taste

1. Heat the olive oil in a 3-quart saucepan. Add the onion and green pepper and sauté until limp.

2. Add the garlic and sauté a minute more.

3. Mix the tomato paste with the water and add this mixture to the pan.

4. Add the sugar, oregano, basil, and cumin. Bring to a boil, reduce heat to low, and simmer uncovered, stirring occasionally until thickened—about 20 to 30 minutes. Add salt and pepper to taste.

5. Serve hot with the Fried Calamari in individual dipping bowls.

Cuban Stomach Remedies

If you have a stomachache in a Cuban household, chances are the abuela of the house will fix you up with one of three popular Cuban remedies. The first line of attack for many families is a thick puree of malanga, the root vegetable that is a staple in Cuban diets.

Another popular option is manzanilla tea, which is not only good for stomach problems—many people swear it cures colds, reduces fevers, and rids the sufferer of headaches.

Still feeling poorly?

The third and final line of attack is Eno®, a brand name for a type of effervescent antacid. It's like the Cuban version of Alka-Seltzer® in powder form. Just mix with water and drink it. Relief is just one good burp away . . .

Croquetas de Pescado
Fish Croquettes

Salt and black pepper to taste
1 pound white fish fillets (or any mild fish)
Water and white wine
4 tablespoons butter
1 cup finely minced onion
⅓ cup flour
1½ cups milk (more or less), at room temperature

¼ teaspoon nutmeg
1 tablespoon dry sherry
1 tablespoon finely chopped parsley
2 tablespoons real mayonnaise
2 tablespoons fresh lemon juice
1 cup dry bread crumbs (more or less)

COATING
2 eggs, beaten with 1 tablespoon water
1 cup dry bread crumbs mixed with
　¼ cup flour

1 teaspoon salt
½ teaspoon black pepper
Vegetable oil for frying

Glenn: A great starter for any seafood dinner is Croquetas de Pescado, or fish croquettes.

Jorge: These ARE NOT those less than appetizing fish sticks you may remember from your days in that low-budget boarding school or the Marine Corps.

Glenn: Sorry Mrs. Paul, but we believe old Mr. Paul would have liked ours a lot better.

Jorge: The best fish croquettes have a crispy shell and a moist middle.

Raúl: You need to serve these hot. There is nothing worse than a cold croqueta.

1. Salt and pepper the fish and poach in a little water and white wine until fully cooked and flaky. Let the fish cool and then flake it with a fork.

2. Melt the butter in a 3-quart saucepan; add the onion and sauté until translucent.

3. Gradually whisk in flour to make a roux—add more butter if necessary to make a smooth roux. Gradually whisk in the milk to form a smooth sauce.

4. Continue cooking until the sauce thickens. Whisk in nutmeg, sherry, parsley, mayonnaise, and lemon juice. Fold in the flaked fish and bread crumbs.

5. Let simmer for 5 minutes over low heat, stirring constantly. Taste and season with pepper and salt. Refrigerate this mixture until well chilled—at least 1 hour. *TIP: The mixture needs to be firm enough to form into rolls. If your mixture is too soft or sticky, add some additional bread crumbs.*

6. For the coating, beat the eggs with water in a mixing bowl until frothy. Combine the bread crumbs and flour in a second bowl with salt and pepper.

7. Shape the fish mixture into logs about ¾ inch thick and 3 inches long. Dip the logs in the egg wash and roll the logs in the seasoned bread crumbs. Dip a second time and re-roll in bread crumbs. *IMPORTANT: Cover logs with plastic wrap and refrigerate for 2 to 3 hours. (You may also freeze for later use, or use the freezer to chill them quickly.)*

8. Get a large frying pan and add enough vegetable oil to cover half the croqueta at a time. Heat the oil to the frying stage—about 350 degrees F.

(continued on page 82)

(continued from page 81)

9. Fry the croquetas in the hot oil, a few at a time for 3 to 4 minutes, turning occasionally, until golden brown. Remove from oil and drain on paper towels.

10. Serve hot with a lemon garnish.

Makes about a dozen croquetas

Croquetas de Pollo
Chicken Croquettes

4 tablespoons butter
¾ cup finely minced onion
4 cups ground cooked chicken meat, white or dark
1 tablespoon fresh lime juice
2 tablespoons finely chopped cilantro
⅓ cup flour

1½ cups milk (more or less), at room temperature
¼ teaspoon nutmeg
1 tablespoon dry sherry
1 cup dry bread crumbs (more or less)
Salt and black pepper to taste

COATING

2 eggs, beaten with 1 tablespoon water
1 cup dry bread crumbs mixed with ¼ cup flour

1 teaspoon salt
½ teaspoon pepper
Vegetable oil for frying

1. In a large pan, melt the butter; add onion, and sauté until translucent.

2. Grind the cooked chicken in a food processor. Add fresh lime juice and grind in chopped cilantro for a nice flavor twist.

3. Stir flour into butter and onion mixture to make a roux—add more butter if necessary to make a smooth roux. Gradually whisk in the milk to form a smooth sauce. Continue cooking until the sauce thickens. Your sauce needs to be very thick, almost like wallpaper paste. Whisk in the nutmeg and sherry. Fold in the ground chicken and bread crumbs.

4. Let simmer for 5 minutes on low heat. Taste and season with salt and pepper. Refrigerate this mixture until well chilled—at least 1 hour. *NOTE: The mixture needs to be firm enough to form into rolls. If your mixture is too soft or sticky, add some additional bread crumbs.*

5. Shape the chicken mixture into logs about ¾ inch thick and 3 inches long.

6. For the coating, make an egg wash by beating the eggs with water until frothy in a small bowl. Combine the bread crumbs and flour in a second bowl; add salt and pepper.

7. Dip the logs in the egg wash and roll the logs in the seasoned bread crumbs. Dip a second time and re-roll in bread crumbs. *IMPORTANT: Cover logs with plastic wrap and refrigerate for 2 to 3 hours. (You may also freeze for later use, or use the freezer to chill them quickly.)*

8. Fry the croquetas in hot oil—about 350 degrees F, a few at a time, 3 to 4 minutes, turning occasionally, until golden brown. Remove from oil and drain on paper towels. You may also cook them in a deep-fat fryer, following manufacturer's directions.

Makes about a dozen croquetas

Jorge: We love to serve finger foods at parties.

Glenn: They help contribute to a casual, party atmosphere.

Raúl: And finger foods mean fewer dishes to wash when the party is over.

Glenn: There is nothing easier than washing your fingers!

Jorge: The nice thing about croquetas is that you can make them a day or two ahead and cook them in a few minutes on the stovetop.

Empanadas de Espinaca
Spinach Empanadas

Jorge: They say that Cubans and green vegetables don't mix!

Glenn: Very few classic Cuban recipes include green vegetables.

Raúl: But that doesn't mean that we never ate green vegetables in Cuba. We frequently ate string beans, okra, and green peas at our house.

Jorge: However, I don't remember eating very much spinach in Cuba.

Glenn: This dish is a favorite in Spain, where they evidently eat more spinach than Popeye.

3 cups fresh spinach, chopped
⅓ cup olive oil
4 cloves garlic, finely chopped
1½ cups Roma tomatoes, seeded, peeled and chopped

4 hard-boiled eggs, chopped
1 tablespoon fresh lemon juice
Salt and pepper to taste

DOUGH

2 cups flour
½ teaspoon salt
1 teaspoon baking powder
2 tablespoons butter

4 tablespoons lard (or substitute vegetable shortening)
1 whole egg plus 1 egg yolk
½ cup cold water (more or less)

1. Steam the spinach in a steamer until wilted, but not mushy—just a minute or two in the steamer.

2. Heat the olive oil in a sauté pan. When it is moderately hot, quickly stir in the garlic and tomatoes, stirring constantly, just for a couple minutes. Remove the pan from heat and let cool. Mix in the cooked spinach.

3. Finally, gently fold in the chopped hard-boiled eggs. Add the lemon juice. Salt and pepper the mixture to taste.

FOR THE DOUGH

1. Sift the flour with salt and baking powder. Place half the flour mixture in a large mixing bowl. Make a well in the center. Place the butter, lard, eggs, and water in the well. Mix at low speed to form a paste.

2. Continue to mix in the flour mixture until all is added. You may need to add water—slowly and in small quantities—until the dough reaches the right consistency. The dough should be soft and pliable, like pie dough.

3. Place the dough in a bowl, cover with a plastic wrap and refrigerate for 30 minutes.

4. Lightly flour a work surface. Divide the dough into 4 pieces (keep the pieces you aren't using in the refrigerator until you need them); use a floured rolling pin to roll out the dough about ⅛ inch thick.

(continued on page 86)

(continued from page 84)

5. Use a large round cookie cutter or bowl (about 4 inches in diameter) to cut perfect circles from the dough. Use a slotted spoon (to allow any excess liquid to drain from the filling) and put some filling in the center of the circle and fold over to make a half circle. Don't over-fill.

6. Seal the edges of the dough with your fingers or a fork to make a scalloped edge.

7. Get a large frying pan and add enough vegetable oil to cover the empanadas completely. Heat the oil to the frying stage—about 350 degrees F.

8. Fry the empanadas in the oil, turning occasionally until brown on all sides. Drain on paper towels. Serve hot.

9. You may also bake these in the oven on a lightly greased baking sheet at 350 degrees F for approximately 15 to 20 minutes, or until golden brown.

TIP: There are always several people in any crowd who will lose their composure at the simple mention of the word "spinach." For best results, just tell your guests that these are "Spanish" empanadas. The reaction usually goes like this: "These empanadas are great! What? That's spinach? But I hate spinach!"

Serves 6 to 8 (Makes 14 to 18 empanadas)

CUBAN "SQUARE DANCING"

Yes, Cubans have their own version of square dancing, without the typical barn and hay accompaniments that seem to go hand-in-hand with the American-style dance. Called Rueda, the dance was initially developed in Havana in the 1950s. Based on traditional salsa dancing, Rueda is danced by groups of couples in a large circle or wheel (hence the name).

As in square dancing, a "caller" announces many different dance moves. Each move has its own name and many have hand signals associated
with them—an important consideration in loud clubs where not all of the dancers might hear the "calls."

Some of the moves demonstrate a real sense of humor. One move simulates "diving" into a pool. Another popular move, besala tres veces "kiss her three times," is very popular. This one sends you across the circle to kiss someone else's partner.

Aficionados are always developing new moves. The "balsero," or rafter, simulates ocean waves.

There is even a move that mimics talking on a cell phone.

Watching a rueda is like watching a kaleidoscope—everyone is in constant motion moving this way and that, changing partners, changing moves—it's all very precise. There are many places in Miami that teach rueda along with traditional salsa dancing and it has become very popular with Miami teens.

Huevos Cubano
Cuban Deviled Eggs

8 hard-boiled eggs
1 tablespoon mayonnaise
½ teaspoon salt
½ teaspoon pepper

SAUCE
¾ cup minced onion
¾ cup minced green bell pepper
Olive oil for sautéing

1 teaspoon mustard powder
1 cup grated sharp cheddar cheese
1 teaspoon fresh lime juice

3 cloves garlic, minced
1 (16-ounce) can tomato sauce
Chopped cilantro leaves

1. Preheat oven to 400 degrees F.

2. Peel the hard-boiled eggs and cut in half lengthwise. Remove the yolks.

3. In a small bowl, mash the yolks and add mayonnaise to make a thick paste. Mash in salt, pepper, mustard powder, half the cheese, and lime juice.

4. Taste and adjust seasoning as necessary.

5. Use a spoon to place the yolk mixture back into the egg halves.

6. Make the sauce by sautéing the onion and green pepper in olive oil until limp. Add the minced garlic and sauté an additional 2 minutes.

7. Stir in the tomato sauce and cook briefly. Taste the sauce and add salt and pepper as necessary.

8. Place the stuffed eggs in a lightly buttered shallow baking dish or cake pan. Pour the sauce over the stuffed eggs and sprinkle with remaining cheese.

9. Bake for about 15 minutes until the cheese melts and browns slightly. Sprinkle the top of the dish with fresh chopped cilantro leaves.

10. Serve hot over rice or with bread or toast.

Serves 8

Jorge: Huevos Cubano is the Cuban version of deviled eggs.

Glenn: However, you don't serve these eggs as a cold appetizer, but as a delicious hot dish that you can serve at a brunch or even as the main entrée at a meal.

Jorge: We traditionally serve the dish over white rice. However, it tastes great alone with a side of toasted Cuban bread.

Raúl: Put out a dish of Huevos Cubano with a tray of Cuban bread and watch it disappear.

Gambas al Ajillo
Garlic Shrimp

Glenn: For cocktail or evening parties, we like to serve a large selection of tapas, or Spanish-style appetizers.

Raúl: Cubans call these "bocaditos" or little bites. The idea is the same—just a small serving of something served as an appetizer or a "grazing" food at parties.

Jorge: Gambas al Ajillo is the classic tapas dish of Spain. In Madrid, every restaurant serves a version of this dish.

¼ cup olive oil
1 pound shrimp, cleaned, deveined, and butterflied
5 cloves garlic, mashed
½ teaspoon salt

1½ teaspoons sweet Spanish paprika
1 teaspoon ground cumin
Fresh lemon juice
1 tablespoon minced parsley

1. Heat the olive oil in a large sauté pan. Add the shrimp and continue sautéing. When the shrimp begins to cook on one side, about 2 to 3 minutes, turn it over in the pan.

2. Let cook a minute or two, no more. Add the garlic, salt, paprika, and cumin, and lightly toss the shrimp in the pan several times. You want to keep cooking just long enough to bring the flavor out of the garlic.

3. Sprinkle the shrimp with some fresh lemon juice and parsley.

4. Serve hot with plenty of Cuban bread for soaking up the delicious garlic oil.

Serves 4 to 8

Escabeche de Pescado
Marinated Fish

2 pounds kingfish or white fish, cleaned
    and scaled
Salt and pepper to taste

MARINADE
2 cups olive oil
2 cups vinegar
1½ teaspoons salt
½ teaspoon pepper

Flour
Olive oil

2 teaspoons oregano
4 cups chopped onions
4 cups chopped green bell pepper

1. Cut the fish into ruedas ("wheels" in Spanish, but what Anglos would call "steaks"). Salt and pepper the fish pieces and dredge in flour.

2. Fry the fish in medium-hot olive oil until brown on both sides and cooked through.

3. Place the fish in a large crockery pot or bowl, anything large enough to hold everything, as long as it is non-metallic.

4. For the marinade, whisk together the oil and vinegar and add salt, pepper, and oregano in a large bowl.

5. Cover the fish in the pot with the onions and green peppers. Pour the oil and vinegar sauce over the top.

6. Cover the pot and place in the refrigerator. You need to marinate the fish at least 2 days before serving.

7. Serve cold with crackers or bread. You may also heat this in a saucepan and serve it hot over white rice.

Serves 8 to 10

Glenn: Raúl eats more escabeche than anyone I know.

Raúl: I catch many fish, and this is a great way to enjoy them. The kingfish is probably the best fish to use in this recipe.

Jorge: However, you can also use just about any good-size white fish, even tuna or salmon!

Glenn: There are several ways to eat this. For a party, we usually serve it cold with crackers or bread or you can heat it briefly in a saucepan and serve it hot over rice.

Pasta de Pollo
Chicken Spread

2 cups cubed cooked chicken
⅓ cup mayonnaise
8 ounces cream cheese
½ teaspoon ground cumin
3 cloves garlic, minced

½ cup minced sweet onion
½ cup chopped black olives
½ cup chopped green olives
Salt and freshly ground pepper

1. Place the chicken, mayonnaise, cream cheese, and cumin in a food processor and process until coarsely chopped.

2. Place the mixture in a mixing bowl. Fold in garlic, onion, and olives by hand. Salt and pepper to taste.

3. Serve with crackers.

Serves 6 to 8

Jorge: Pastes like this one are a traditional spread served on crackers.

Glenn: For parties, Jorge likes to get a little fancy and make attractive little canapés with this spread on individual crackers.

Raúl: Or do it Raúl-style and just serve it in a bowl with Cuban crackers or bread on the side.

Ensalada de Huevos
Egg Salad

Glenn: Cuban-style egg salad makes a great party appetizer.

Jorge: We like to serve it on creatively cut slices of Cuban toast.

Raúl: Made with Cuban bread, of course.

Glenn: The best way to eat these is with warm toast and cold egg salad. So put these together just before serving.

12 hard-boiled eggs, peeled and chopped
⅓ cup finely chopped celery
⅓ cup finely chopped sweet pickles
⅔ teaspoon dry mustard
⅔ teaspoon ground cumin
1 tablespoon fresh lime juice
½ cup mayonnaise (more or less)
Salt and pepper to taste
2 gloves garlic, finely minced
4 tablespoons butter, softened
1 loaf Cuban or French bread
Sweet Spanish paprika

1. Use a large knife or cleaver to chop up the eggs thoroughly. Add celery, pickles, mustard, cumin, lime juice, mayonnaise, and salt and pepper. Stir until just mixed. Adjust the amount of mayonnaise to your taste. The same goes for the salt and pepper, start easy and taste it. Chill. (We mean the salad, but if you're feeling uptight or anxious, you can chill too.)

2. Use a fork to mash the minced garlic into the butter.

3. Slice the bread in ½-inch-thick slices. Compress the bread slices with a bacon press, rolling pin, frying pan, or whatever you have handy. The idea is to smash the bread down to about one-third of its original thickness. If you have your own plancha (Cuban sandwich press), you can make your toast and compress it all at the same time.

4. Butter the compressed bread slices with the garlic butter, and toast briefly under a low broiler, turning once, until golden brown on both sides.

5. Cut the bread into triangles, squares, rectangles, or any other geometric shape that grabs you. Impress your friends with a precisely cut trapezoid or parallelogram! In any case, the idea is to make small canapés that you can serve as an appetizer.

6. Just before serving, spread the chilled egg salad on the warm toast.

7. Lay the small toast shapes out on a serving tray and dust very lightly with sweet paprika.

Serves 8 to 10

Pizza Cubana
Cuban Pizza

Jorge: Cuban pizzas combine the traditional tastes of Italy with a few Cuban variations, things like plátanos, picadillo, Spanish chorizo, and lobster.

Glenn: The Cuban style of pizza was born in Havana, but perfected at several shops in the beach town of Varadero.

Raúl: Pizza in the Varadero style is the most popular in Miami, with a thicker crust, a heavier sauce, and a cheese blend that packs a little more bite.

Jorge: In Cuba, Gouda cheese was widely available and that's the cheese they used for pizza.

Glenn: In Miami, most Cuban pizza places use a blend of half Gouda and half mozzarella.

Jorge: While working on our own Cuban pizza recipe, Glenn came up with the idea for a "white" Cuban pizza.

Raúl: It doesn't look white — it's green!

Glenn: OK, maybe it's not 100 percent authentic, but it tastes great.

DOUGH
1 tablespoon sugar
1 package yeast
1 cup warm water (110 degrees F)
2½ to 3¼ cups white flour
1 teaspoon salt
2 tablespoons olive oil

SAUCE
1 cup finely chopped green bell pepper
1 cup finely chopped onion
¼ cup olive oil
4 cloves garlic
1 teaspoon salt
1 (28-ounce) can tomato puree
1 tablespoon lemon juice
1½ tablespoons sugar
1 teaspoon paprika
1 teaspoon ground oregano
½ teaspoon ground bay leaf

TOPPINGS
1 cup Gouda cheese, grated (more or less) plus 1 cup mozzarella cheese, grated (more or less), blended together

PICK ONE OR MORE OF THE FOLLOWING:
Spanish chorizo, sliced very thin "pepperoni style" or ground in a food processor or meat grinder
Portuguese chorizo
Diced ham
Cooked shrimp (olive oil, salt, pepper, and ground cumin—see Toppings, page 101)
Cooked lobster (olive oil, salt, pepper, and ground cumin—see Toppings, page 101)
Ripe plantains
Picadillo
Leftover lechón asado
Veggies: green bell pepper, mushrooms, onions, chopped garlic, black olives, green olives, red or green tomato slices

FOR THE DOUGH
1. Dissolve the sugar and yeast in the water in a small bowl. Let stand for 10 minutes in a warm place—it should begin to foam.

2. Sift together the flour and the salt. Place the yeast mixture and the olive oil in the bowl of a stand mixer with the dough hook attached. Turn the mixer to low and gradually add the flour, a little at a time, until you have a stiff, but pliable dough. Adjust the amount of flour, more or less, to achieve the right consistency.

(continued on page 99)

(continued from page 96)

3. Let the machine knead the dough for about 2 to 3 minutes. Place this smooth ball of dough into a greased bowl, cover, and set aside in a warm place to rise until double in size, about 45 minutes to 1 hour. (If you do use a stand mixer, skip the next 2 steps.)

4. If you don't have a stand mixer, don't despair! You can easily mix the dough with a wooden spoon. Gradually add the flour, a little at a time, until you have a stiff, but pliable dough. Adjust the amount of flour, more or less, to achieve the right consistency.

5. Knead the dough with your hands for approximately 10 minutes on a lightly floured surface. Fold the dough in half, knead, dust lightly with flour, and repeat this step about a dozen times. Properly kneaded dough will be smooth and not sticky.

FOR THE SAUCE:

1. Use a large saucepan and sauté the green peppers and onion in olive oil until limp. Add the garlic and sauté an additional minute or two, stirring constantly.

2. Add the salt, tomato puree, lemon juice, sugar, paprika, oregano, and bay leaf.

3. Bring to a boil, reduce heat to low and simmer, uncovered, stirring occasionally, until the sauce thickens, about 20 to 30 minutes.

4. Remove the sauce from the heat and let cool. Remove bay leaf.

TO MAKE THE PIZZAS:

1. Preheat the oven to 400 degrees F.

2. Punch down the dough. Remove it from the bowl and place on a lightly floured surface. Divide dough into 4 pieces. Work out the dough by hand to form 4 individual rounds, about 6 inches in diameter. Turn and re-flour the dough as you form the crusts. The crust should be quite thick—about ½ inch.

3. Place the individual pizza rounds on a well-greased baking sheet. Liberally cover the dough with the sauce. Add your favorite topping (or toppings) and cover the pizza with the cheese.

4. Bake in the oven for approximately 14 to 18 minutes. The cheese should be melted and starting to brown slightly at the edges of the pizzas.

Makes 4 personal-size pizzas, serves 6 to 8 as an appetizer

Pizza Cubana Blanca en el Estilo de Glenn— Glenn's White Cuban Pizza

Dough recipe (see page 96)

Pesto Sauce

1 tablespoon lemon juice

4 cloves garlic

¾ cup olive oil

¼ cup pine nuts

1½ cups cilantro leaves and stems

1 cup grated fresh Parmesan cheese

Dash ground black pepper

Toppings

4 large mild Anaheim chiles

6 red ripe Roma tomatoes, sliced

1 cup Gouda cheese, grated (more or less) plus 1 cup mozzarella cheese, grated (more or less), blended together

OPTIONAL:

Portuguese chorizo or Spanish chorizo sliced very thin or ground in a food processor or meat grinder

For the Dough

1. Follow the "Dough" instructions on page 96 and form the individual pizzas.

For the Sauce

1. Place the lemon juice, garlic, olive oil, pine nuts, and cilantro in a blender or food processor. Blend on high until you have a smooth puree.

2. Add the Parmesan cheese and pulse the blender a few times to incorporate. Add a little freshly ground black pepper to taste.

For the Toppings

1. Buy mild Anaheim chiles—they are long and quite large and are light green in color. Roast the chiles under the broiler, turning once, so that the skins are blackened. Let cool slightly.

2. Hold the chiles under cold running water. Remove the top, stems, and seeds—discard. Peel away the charred black skin.

3. Slice the chile lengthwise and flatten. Cut into pieces about 1-inch square.

4. This pizza is best with just the chiles, tomatoes, and cheese. If you really need the meat, use Spanish or Portuguese chorizo.

To make the pizzas

1. Preheat the oven to 400 degrees F.

2. Follow the instructions on page 99 to make and form the pizza rounds.

3. Place the individual pizza rounds on a well-greased baking sheet.

4. Liberally cover the dough with the pesto sauce. Sprinkle on some chiles and sliced tomatoes. Cover each pizza with the cheese.

5. Bake in the oven for approximately 14 to 18 minutes. The cheese should be melted and starting to brown slightly at the edges of the pizzas.

Makes 4 personal-size pizzas, serves 6 to 8 as an appetizer

TOPPINGS

Chorizo—the classic Cuban pizza is made with Spanish chorizo. Most pizza places tend to grind this dry sausage to the consistency of taco meat. Use a meat grinder or a food processor with the metal chopping blade. You may also use it "pepperoni style," sliced thin in rounds. Whichever style you use, spread evenly over the sauce and under the cheese.

Portuguese chorizo—available in many markets. The spices are similar; however, this sausage is not as dry and is more tender than Spanish chorizo. It makes a great topping for pizza.

Diced ham—also very popular. Use a good quality ham slice and cut it into bite-size pieces.

Shrimp and lobster—when we add shrimp or lobster (and sometimes both) to our pizzas, we like to sauté them first in a little olive oil. Remove the lobster meat from the tails and cut into chunks. Peel and devein the shrimp. Season the shrimp or lobster lightly with salt, pepper, and a little cumin. Sauté the shrimp or lobster pieces, flipping once after a minute or so, until they turn pink, about 3 minutes. Do not overcook!

Plantains—use very ripe plantains cut lengthwise in strips about ½ inch thick. Some people also use sweet ripe yellow bananas. If using plantain or banana, add to the top of the pizza during the last 5 or 6 minutes of baking. Arrange the slices on top

of the cheese. They will soften and brown slightly from the oven heat.

Leftover picadillo and lechón asado—also popular toppings.

Vegetables—Cuban pizzas feature all of the same vegetable toppings that are popular on American pizzas. You should slice your green peppers in rings. Cut your onions in rings and then cut the rings in half. Select one or more of these vegetables or add them all for the ultimate Cuban pizza with everything.

Tamales de Pollo y Tocina
Chicken and Bacon Tamales

8 slices bacon, chopped
1 large onion, finely chopped
1 green bell pepper, finely chopped
¼ cup olive oil
5 cloves garlic, minced
1 teaspoon salt
½ teaspoon freshly ground black pepper
1½ pounds boneless, skinless chicken
   thighs, chopped
½ cup tomato paste
½ cup warm water

½ cup red or white wine
1 tablespoon white vinegar
3 cups ground fresh corn (may substitute
   frozen)
¾ cup lard, butter, or shortening
2½ cups chicken broth
2½ cups masa harina
Dash or two of Bijol for color
Juice of 1 large lemon
Cornhusks (soak dried cornhusks in hot
   water before using)

1. Fry the bacon in a large sauté pan over medium heat until crispy, but not burned. Use a slotted spoon to remove the crispy bacon bits. Try not to eat these as you proceed through the remaining recipe steps.

2. OK, if you think there is a good chance that you may be tempted to eat the crunchy bacon bits, sauté a couple of additional slices of chopped bacon until crispy. Place these crunchy and delicious bacon bits in a separate bowl labeled: "If tempted to eat crunchy bacon bits during recipe preparation, eat these!"

3. Sauté the onion and green pepper in olive oil over medium heat, stirring occasionally, until the onions are soft. Add garlic, salt, and pepper and continue to fry for 2 to 3 minutes. Remove the vegetables from the pan with a slotted spoon. Keep the oil in the pan.

4. Use a meat cleaver to chop the raw chicken into small chunks. Sauté the chicken in the oil in the pan until cooked through. Now place everything back in the pan: the chicken, vegetables, and whatever is left of those crunchy bacon bits.

5. Mix tomato paste in warm water and add it, the wine, and the vinegar to the pan, stirring long enough to blend well. Simmer for about 10 minutes.

6. Slice the corn kernels off a cob of fresh sweet corn until you have 3 cups (or use frozen corn). Quickly grind the corn in a food processor with your choice of fat (lard, butter, or shortening) until you get a very coarse mixture with visible corn kernels. Don't over process.

7. Remove the corn from the processor and place in a large 8-quart stockpot. Blend in warm chicken broth and masa harina. Add a dash of Bijol powder to give it a nice yellow color.

(continued on page 104)

Jorge: The nice thing about tamales is that you can make them several days ahead of time and then just heat them up in a steamer for a quick dinner or a party.

Glenn: Cuban tamales are a great taste treat. In a Cuban tamal, you mix the meat in with the dough. You don't use it as a filling like in Mexican tamales.

Glenn: In our last cookbook, we included a traditional recipe for pork tamales.

Raúl: This recipe is a little different.

Jorge: Chicken tamales are not as common as pork or ham tamales but they are very good. For a little twist, we add smoked bacon to give the tamales some delicious pork flavor.

(continued from page 103)

8. Add the chicken mixture to the mixture in the pot. Add lemon juice, salt, and pepper and stir. Cook over low heat, stirring frequently (don't let it burn) until it thickens, about 20 minutes.

9. Add more masa or more broth as necessary so you have a stiff, but pliable paste. Taste and add salt if needed. Remove from heat and let cool.

10. Take two husks and overlap them flat on the table. Put some of the corn mixture in the center of the cornhusks. Fold the cornhusks, first over the filling the short way, and then folding up the long way from the ends. Tie with a string.

11. The best way to cook tamales is to use a large pot with about 2 inches of water in the bottom. (If you have the little insert that keeps the food off the bottom, great.)

12. Add the tamales, standing them on end and cover the pot. Bring the water to a boil. Reduce heat and simmer/steam about 1½ to 2 hours.

IMPORTANT: Be sure to check the water level occasionally so that the pot doesn't run dry.

TIP: Freshly cooked tamales tend to be a bit mushy. The best way to make tamales is to cook them a day ahead then put them in the refrigerator overnight. Cooling will help the tamales firm up to the proper consistency. The next day, just steam them long enough to heat through. If you'd like to make a large batch and freeze them, always cook the tamales first and then freeze. Usually we can't resist and end up eating a couple of "loose" tamales the same day!

Makes about 18 to 24 medium-size tamales

THE CUBAN "MICROWAVE"

Many people have asked us, "Why don't any of your recipes use a pressure cooker?" No Cuban abuela (grandmother) could live without her pressure cooker—the Cuban microwave. In fact, at Raúl's house, the abuelas frequently argue over whose particular pressure cooker is the best. So many Cubans grew up eating food prepared this way, they just can't conceive of cooking Cuban food without one.

The pressure cooker first became known in the U.S. around 1915, but didn't really take off until Word War II, when it became immensely popular. At the same time, Cuba was falling in love with "all things American" and the pressure cooker became a big hit with home cooks. When metals rationing ended after the war, pressure cooker manufacturers flooded the market with poorly designed and poor quality cookers. Many American housewives, including Glenn's mother, had terrible experiences with exploding pressure cookers in the kitchen. In the United States, this growing bad reputation marked the death of the pressure cooker.

However, in Cuba pressure cooking lived on. Raúl's mother and Jorge's mother use their pressure cookers all of the time and for frijoles negros, the taste can't be beat. Foods really do cook faster in the "Cuban microwave." Pressure cookers are also great for tenderizing a cheap cut of meat. However, most Americans do not have pressure cookers and do not want them. That's why we don't use pressure cookers in our recipes, which we designed so that anyone, anywhere, could make Cuban food simply and easily with the equipment that they would have in their home.

Plus we'll let you in on a little secret. Abuelas, please cover your ears now. Many dishes actually taste better without pressure cooking. That's because some dishes end up tasting overcooked and overprocessed when made in the pressure cooker.

Cuban Parties: Nochevieja—New Year's Eve

Glenn: For Cubans, New Year's Eve is more of a dance party than a feast like Christmas. It is a night of music and dancing, eating great foods, and having a great time.

Jorge: New Year's Eve is part of the long celebration of the Christmas Season that begins with Christmas Eve . . .

Raúl: . . . and the preparations for Noche Buena—Christmas Eve—begin days before . . .

Jorge: . . . and ends on Three Kings Day.

Glenn: Something unique to Cuban culture is the tradition of "Año Viejo," the Old Year's man. The children spend the days leading up to New Year's Eve building and dressing the Año Viejo man, a type of scarecrow dressed in old clothes and stuffed with paper, magazines, and anything else that will burn.

Raúl: These giant dolls sit on the front porches of the houses throughout the day waiting for the stroke of midnight.

Jorge: At midnight, everyone carries their Año Viejo man into the street and sets it on fire.

Glenn: Be sure to check your local fire codes before trying this at home!

Raúl: The Año Viejo man represents all the bad things that happened during the past year. By burning the Old Year's man, you are destroying the bad things of the past and welcoming the fresh start of the New Year.

Jorge: It's a fun way for the kids to celebrate and for everyone to say goodbye to the old year.

Raúl: At midnight, it's customary to eat twelve grapes (one for each month) and drink Sidra, a "hard" sparkling apple cider.

Jorge: Just before midnight, each person at the party takes a bunch of 12 grapes.

Glenn: You're supposed to eat one grape with each stroke of the clock chime, so you have to eat them fast. Seedless grapes really come in handy on New Year's!

Jorge: Tradition has it that for every sweet grape you eat, you will have a good month in the New Year.

Glenn: However, if you bite into a bad grape—ouch—that means one BAD month.

Jorge: My sister is always very careful to make sure no one at the party gets a bad grape.

Raul: Hey, don't forget the fireworks.

Jorge: Yes, you can buy fireworks all over Miami during the weeks of Christmas and New Year's. Bottle rockets, firecrackers, and every firework . . .

Raúl: . . . the noisier the better . . .

Jorge: . . . imaginable gets shot off at midnight.

Glenn: Many people wait until the Año Viejo doll is ablaze before setting off the fireworks. It's quite a sight with dolls burning, fireworks exploding, and everyone shouting "¡Próspero Año Nuevo!" or "Happy New Year!"

Raúl: We also have a tradition of taking a bucket of water, running out to the street and dumping it. That's very typical.

Jorge: The symbolism is throwing out the dirty water accumulated over the past year and starting the New Year fresh and clean.

Glenn: Yes and the water comes in handy if one of your fireworks lands in the neighbor's garbage can!

Tortilla Española de Mar
Spanish Seafood Omelet

Glenn: A Spanish tortilla or omelet is nothing like those thin, wimpy, anemic-looking egg dishes you get at the local pancake house.

Jorge: The Spanish tortilla is thick, rich, and full of flavor.

Raúl: Spanish omelets are a favorite of Cubans for breakfast and even lunch. They are truly a meal in themselves.

Glenn: In Spain, many bars serve a hearty tortilla as a tapas item. It also makes a great appetizer for a meal or as a party dish.

1 cup peeled and thinly sliced new potatoes
¼ cup olive oil
1 cup chopped onion
Salt and pepper to taste
1 pound medium shrimp, peeled and deveined
2 (4- to 6-ounce) lobster tails, meat removed from shell and cut in bite-size pieces (you may substitute ½ pound sea scallops cut in bite-size pieces)

½ pound cooked crabmeat
Cumin to taste
12 eggs, beaten with 5 tablespoons soft butter (room temperature)
Pinch of salt
Dash of black pepper
Chopped parsley for garnish

1. The best Spanish tortillas, or omelets, are usually made in a cast-iron frying pan about 10 to 12 inches in diameter and 2 or 3 inches deep. However, any frying or sauté pan deep enough to hold the egg mixture will work nicely.

2. Parboil the potatoes by placing them in a saucepan full of lightly salted water. Bring to a boil, reduce heat to low and simmer until tender—about 15 to 20 minutes. Drain.

3. Heat some olive oil in the pan, and sauté the parboiled potatoes and onions until lightly browned, stirring frequently. Season the potatoes and onions with a little salt and pepper. Remove the potatoes and onions from the pan and set aside.

4. Add a little more oil to the pan and sauté the shrimp, lobster and crabmeat in small batches until just barely cooked though. Lightly salt, pepper, and add cumin to the seafood as you cook it, turning frequently. Don't overcook. It is better to undercook the seafood a bit at this point. Remove seafood from the pan and set aside.

5. There should now be some oil remaining in the pan. For the next step you'll want just enough oil to cover the bottom of the pan, so if there is more than that, drain some off now.

6. In a bowl, beat the eggs with a wire whisk. Add softened butter, whisking vigorously. You will now have little flecks of butter in the egg mixture. Whisk in a pinch of salt and a dash of black pepper. Add potatoes, onions, shrimp, lobster, and crabmeat to the beaten eggs.

7. Heat the remaining oil in the pan to medium-hot. Pour the egg mixture in the pan and cover. Immediately reduce heat to low. Cook for approximately 7 to 10 minutes until the eggs are set and firm.

8. Cover the pan with a large plate and flip. Return to the pan and fry the other side until just lightly browned. Cut the tortilla into 12 wedges and garnish with chopped parsley.

Serves 6 to 8

Sopas
Soups

Guisado de Pollo
Chicken Stew

Glenn: Chicken has always been popular in Cuba. Many people have several chickens in a coop in the backyard for fresh eggs and meat.

Raúl: The next time you have a special occasion, a wedding anniversary, birthday, or Valentine's, why not surprise someone you love with their very own live chicken?

Jorge: Just tie a simple red bow around the chicken's neck.

Glenn: A small bag of cracked corn rounds out this great all-occasion gift.

Raúl: OK, maybe the live chicken idea isn't so great . . .

Jorge: Plan B—Use the chicken to make Guisado de Pollo, one of those dishes that taste even better the day after.

Glenn: So don't be afraid to prepare a day ahead and reheat the next day for a romantic dinner for two.

5 cloves garlic, minced
1 teaspoon salt
1 teaspoon black pepper
2 teaspoons sweet Spanish paprika
2 teaspoons cumin
Olive oil for paste (about 2 tablespoons)
1 whole chicken, bone in and skin on, cut up into pieces (breasts cut in half or thirds)

2 cups chopped onions
2 cups chopped green bell pepper
Olive oil for sautéing
½ cup white wine
1 bay leaf
½ cup chicken stock or broth (more or less)
3 potatoes, peeled and cubed
2 cups frozen green peas
½ cup sliced green olives with pimientos

THE DAY BEFORE

1. Mix the garlic, salt, pepper, paprika, and cumin with a little olive oil to form a thick paste. Rub the paste onto the chicken pieces.

2. Place chicken in a non-metallic bowl or cake pan, cover with plastic wrap, and refrigerate overnight.

COOKING DAY

1. Sauté the onions and green pepper in olive oil in a large frying pan until the vegetables are soft. Remove the vegetables and place in a large saucepan or stockpot.

2. Brown the chicken pieces in the hot oil.

3. Add chicken to the saucepan with wine and bay leaf. Add just enough chicken stock to cover the meat.

4. Bring to a boil; reduce heat to low, and cook 1 hour. Add more chicken stock if the stew becomes too thick.

5. Add the cubed potatoes and continue cooking until the potatoes are soft, about 20 to 30 minutes.

6. Taste and add salt as necessary.

7. Is the stew too thin? Make a paste of cornstarch and water and stir rapidly into the stew.

8. Fifteen minutes before serving, add the peas and olives.

Serves 4

Sopa de Cebolla
Onion Soup

4 tablespoons butter
4 tablespoons olive oil
3 cups thin-sliced yellow onions
2 cloves garlic, minced
4 cups beef stock or broth
¼ cup dry sherry

½ teaspoon black pepper
Salt to taste
Cuban bread, sliced thick and toasted (one or two slices per bowl)
Grated white melting cheese (asadero, Gouda, Monterey Jack, mozzarella, etc.)

1. Melt the butter in the olive oil in a large saucepan. Fry the onions until translucent.

2. Add the garlic and sauté 1 minute more.

3. Add the beef stock or broth, sherry, and black pepper. Bring to a boil; reduce heat to low, and simmer, uncovered, for 25 minutes. Adjust seasonings to taste—now is the time to add some salt.

4. To serve, place a slice or two of toasted Cuban bread in each bowl.

5. Sprinkle grated cheese (be generous) on top of each slice of bread. Pour the hot soup over the bread (thus melting the cheese) and serve immediately.

Serves 4

Glenn: Onion soup is so easy to make and always tastes great.

Jorge: If you grew up eating the onion soup that comes dried in the little packets, you are in for a treat.

Raúl: This is one dish where sweeter onions, such as a Vidalia or a Walla Walla sweet onion, work best.

Glenn: The milder flavor keeps the onions from being too overwhelming.

THE ALLURE OF CANNED VEGETABLES

In Cuba, canned vegetables were essential staples of the home pantry. Canned asparagus and especially canned peas, known as "petit pois" were the most popular. Although the petit pois pea is just a standard pea picked when it is young and slightly sweeter, the name in Cuba became synonymous with the best peas. It may

have been the fancy French name, or just the allure of something "imported" from another country, but Cubans considered canned petit pois peas as the ultimate pea!

You may notice that we usually don't call for canned asparagus or peas in our recipes. We have so many fresh vegetables available in Miami we

just don't have to resort to using canned vegetables. If you grew up in a Cuban household and want to duplicate the authentic flavors you remember, feel free to use your favorite canned vegetables in any recipe. We won't tell a soul.

Sopa de Crema de Queso
Cheese Soup

Glenn: In Minnesota and Wisconsin, everyone eats beer cheese soup, a creamy combination of sharp cheddar cheese and beer. It's a great dish on a cold day. For some reason, they always serve it with fresh popcorn on top.

Raúl: In Miami, where the days are never cold and rarely even cool, we enjoy our own cheese soup. There is no beer in it—although that might not be a bad idea! I'm not so sure about the popcorn though!

Jorge: We make Sopa de Crema de Queso with a cheese that is very popular in Cuba: Gouda cheese, a great tasting cheese that melts easily and makes a deliciously rich soup.

Glenn: The perfect place to dip your slice of freshly baked Cuban bread.

4 tablespoons butter
2 teaspoons finely minced onion
1 clove garlic, minced
3 tablespoons flour
½ cup chicken broth

1½ cups milk at room temperature
6 ounces grated Gouda cheese
1 cup heavy cream
Salt and pepper to taste

1. Melt the butter in a saucepan. Add the onion and garlic and sauté briefly over medium-low heat. (This is one of the very few times we will ever ask you to go easy on the garlic. You need just a small clove, about ½ teaspoon minced.)

2. Next, quickly stir in the flour to make a paste. Add the chicken broth, whisking vigorously to avoid any lumps.

3. Continue whisking and quickly add the milk. Bring almost to a boil, stirring constantly.

4. Add the cheese and use a spoon to continue stirring until the cheese melts completely and blends into the soup.

5. Reduce heat to low and stir in the cream. Let the soup come back up to serving temperature, however do not let it boil! Salt and pepper to taste.

6. Serve hot with plenty of fresh Cuban bread or any non-Cuban bread you may be saddled with in your part of the country.

Serves 4

Sopa de Frijoles Española
Spanish Bean Soup

Jorge: Hearty soups are very popular in all Latin cultures.

Raúl: Many of the best Cuban soups came from Spain, the mother country.

Glenn: One in particular, Sopa de Frijoles Española, is a great, robust dish you can serve as a starter or as the main course.

Jorge: A nice way to finish this dish at the table is with a shot of fresh lime juice.

4 slices smoked bacon, chopped
1½ cups chopped onion
1 cup chopped green bell pepper
3 cloves garlic, mashed
2 tablespoons flour
½ pound ham, cut in chunks
¼ teaspoon ground bay leaf
1 tablespoon ground cumin

1 teaspoon salt
Pinch of Bijol powder
4½ cups chicken broth
2 (16-ounce) cans garbanzo beans, drained
2 cups peeled and cubed potatoes
4 Spanish-style chorizos, casings removed and sliced thick

1. Sauté bacon, onion, and green pepper until the vegetables are limp. Add garlic and sauté for 1 additional minute. Stir in flour to thicken.

2. Place onion mixture in a large stockpot with ham, ground bay leaf, cumin, salt, Bijol powder, and chicken broth. Bring to boil. Cover, reduce heat, and cook for 30 minutes.

3. Add the garbanzo beans to the pot and continue simmering, covered, approximately 1 hour. Stir occasionally and add more chicken broth if the soup gets too thick.

4. Add potatoes and chorizos and cover.

5. Simmer over low heat until potatoes are fork tender, approximately 30 to 40 minutes. Take a cup of the soup out of the pot and mash the beans with a fork in a small bowl. Add the mashed beans back to the pot to thicken the soup.

6. As unlikely as it may seem, many people like to add a squirt or two of fresh lime juice to this dish at the table. If this seems like something that might appeal to you, go ahead. Nobody's looking.

Serves 6

Sopa del Mar
Seafood Soup

Glenn: This is a soup with a split personality. You can make it very cheaply using mostly fish.

Jorge: Or you can really let loose and make it extravagantly with plenty of great seafood.

Raúl: Guess which way we like best?

Jorge: Adjust the seafood mixture any way you wish, or to fit your budget.

Glenn: We like to go the cheap route when the in-laws are coming over for dinner.

Jorge: Always let your conscience be your guide!

1 pound shrimp, peeled and deveined, shells reserved
2 quarts lightly salted water (to make shrimp stock)
Olive oil for sautéing
4 cups chopped onions
3 cups peeled, chopped tomatoes
5 cloves garlic, minced
1 cup thinly sliced carrots
1 cup red potatoes, peeled and cubed

½ cup wine
1 teaspoon Bijol powder
1½ cups bread cubes
2 cloves garlic, minced
3 pounds fish fillets, cut in bite-size pieces (we like to use grouper, mahi-mahi, tuna, or swordfish)
2 (6-ounce) lobster tails, shell on, cut in chunks
1 pound scallops

1. Make a stock by boiling the shells of the shrimp in lightly salted water. Strain and reserve the stock.

2. Use a large saucepot or stockpot. Add some olive oil to the pan and sauté the onions until limp. Add the tomatoes and garlic and cook an additional 2 minutes, stirring constantly. Add the carrots, potatoes, wine, Bijol powder, and the strained stock.

3. Bring to a rolling boil; reduce heat to low and simmer, uncovered, for 45 minutes to 1 hour.

4. Using a frying pan, sauté some bread cubes in a little olive oil. Season the cubes as they sauté with some salt, pepper, and minced garlic, tossing and turning occasionally. Set aside.

5. Heat some more olive oil in the frying pan and sauté the fish, lobster, scallops, and shrimp in small batches until fully cooked. (Shrimp should be pink and firm and the fish white and flaky.)

6. Just before serving, add the sautéed seafood to the soup stock.

7. You also can make individual servings and divide the seafood fairly by spooning equal measures of seafood into individual soup bowls and ladling in the soup stock to fill.

8. Top the soup with the fried bread cubes and serve hot.

Serves 6 to 8

Sopa de Plátanos Maduro
Sweet Plantain Soup

Glenn: There is a Cuban soup made with green plantains that is a traditional favorite.

Jorge: We occasionally make this version, which uses ripe, sweet plantains.

Raúl: Many people eat this for the holidays, especially Thanksgiving.

Jorge: It seems to fit the general feeling of the holiday season when so many things are sweet and rich.

Glenn: One secret? Make sure that your plantains are very ripe—the skin should be nearly black and the flesh soft.

4 large ripe plantains, peeled
Butter for sautéing
2 cloves garlic, minced
4 cups chicken stock or broth

1 tablespoon lemon juice
¼ cup brown sugar
Salt to taste

1. Peel and cut the ripe plantain into 3-inch-thick slices. In a large saucepan, sauté the plantain in a little melted butter until lightly browned on all sides. Add the minced garlic and continue cooking just a minute or two longer.

2. Let the plantains cool for safe handling and use a food processor, blender, or electric mixer to puree them completely.

3. Place the puree back into the saucepan and gradually add the chicken stock, lemon juice, and brown sugar, mixing thoroughly.

4. Bring to a boil, reduce heat to low, and simmer for about 20 minutes.

5. Season with salt. Taste it. Adjust seasonings as necessary. Serve hot.

Serves 4

CUBAN PARTIES: EL DÍA DE AÑO NUEVO—NEW YEAR'S DAY

Glenn: After a wild New Year's Eve party, New Year's Day is a very laid back affair. People tend to sleep a little later, move a little slower, talk a little quieter. . .

Raúl: Cubans talking quietly? You have to be kidding.

Glenn: Let's just say that the overall decibel level is greatly subdued.

Jorge: On New Year's Day, breakfast is strictly optional. Many don't have the stomach for it after drinking too much sidra . . .

Raúl: Hey, stop looking at me like that!

Jorge: . . . and the rest of us are probably still too full from the previous evening's festivities.

Raúl: They say that the favorite Cuban breakfast on New Year's Day is Eno®, a stomach remedy that's a lot like Alka-Seltzer®.

Glenn: Eno is a popular Cuban remedy for the day after the night before. For those who like a remedy that goes down a lot easier and doesn't leave that horrible medicinal aftertaste, we have also included a traditional Cuban hangover recipe, torrejas, in the Desserts chapter.

Raúl: If you want to spend your New Year's Day like a Cuban, here's what you need to do.

Glenn: Well, you could just crank up the TV and watch football all day until someone snaps you out of your flying pigskin-induced stupor.

Raúl: Oh man, it's so hard to walk away from an exciting game!

Glenn: But the Cuban New Year's Day is all about family. So let's do it right . . .

Jorge: Set up some tables and chairs outside on the patio.

Glenn: Unless you live in a Northern climate— then you'll want to set those tables up near a warm fire.

Jorge: Set out some snacks and cold drinks. Put some Cuban music on the sound system and get ready to play games.

Glenn: That's right—in Cuba it is common to play games on New Year's Day.

Jorge: In Cuba, we all gathered together to play board games, dominos, Chinese checkers, Parcheesi, and cubilete—a Cuban dice game.

Glenn: Raúl is the master at Chinese checkers, so if he shows up at your party, watch out!

Potaje de Lentejas y Garbanzos
Potage of Lentils and Garbanzos

Glenn: There's something about a good hot soup that gets the blood flowing and gets everyone talking . . .

Raúl: . . . in between slurping . . .

Glenn: . . . and soon everyone is in a party mood.

Raúl: This recipe is a classic from Spain.

Jorge: But it also has its origins in another culture—the Arabic people who once occupied Spain.

2 cups chopped yellow onion
3 medium Spanish chorizo links, sliced in bite-size chunks
1 cup chopped green bell pepper
Olive oil for frying
5 cloves garlic, peeled and chopped
1 tablespoon white flour
2 quarts chicken broth or stock
¼ cup red wine
1 (28-ounce) can tomatoes, seeded, drained, and chopped

1 cup lentils, rinsed
2 cups canned garbanzos, drained
2 teaspoons salt
1 teaspoon black pepper
1 teaspoon ground cumin
1 bay leaf
1 teaspoon ground cinnamon
Juice of 1 lime
1 cup chopped fresh cilantro leaves
Cornstarch to thicken
Lime wedges and cilantro for garnish

1. In a large pot, sauté the onion, chorizo, and green pepper in olive oil until the onions are limp. Add the garlic and sauté 2 minutes more, stirring constantly.

2. Add the flour and stir vigorously to mix the flour with the oil and vegetables in the pan.

3. Add the chicken broth, wine, tomatoes, lentils, garbanzos, salt, pepper, cumin, bay leaf, and cinnamon.

4. Bring to a boil, reduce heat to low, and simmer for about 2 hours.

5. About 15 minutes before serving, remove the bay leaf, stir in the lime juice and the cilantro leaves. Add a little cornstarch mixed with water to thicken the soup slightly.

6. Serve in bowls garnished with cilantro sprigs and lime wedges.

   TIP: Loud music played during the soup course will keep those distracting slurping noises to a minimum.

Serves 6

Platos Principales

Main Dishes

Arroz Frito con Lechón Asado
Cuban Fried Rice

Jorge: There are many Chinese people in Cuba.

Raúl: In fact, at one time Havana boasted the largest Chinatown in Latin America.

Glenn: The Chinese had an influence on Cuban cooking. In fact, in Cuba they call soy sauce "salsa china." Arroz Frito is probably one of the best examples of Chinese-Cuban cross culture.

Jorge: After a pig roast or when we make a large lechón, we frequently use the leftover pork meat to make this delicious version of fried rice.

Raúl: This recipe is the standard—with a few variations—for the arroz frito sold in Cuban restaurants all over Miami.

6 eggs
1 tablespoon soy sauce
2 tablespoons chicken stock or broth
Peanut or vegetable oil for frying
1 cup chopped onion
1 cup chopped green bell pepper
3 cloves garlic, minced

4 cups cooked rice
½ cup chicken stock or broth (more or less) mixed with 2 tablespoons soy sauce
2 cups diced leftover lechón asado (or substitute ham)
½ cup chopped green onions
½ cup frozen green peas

1. Scramble the eggs with a whisk, adding soy sauce and chicken broth.

2. Heat a tablespoon or two of oil in a 5-quart or larger sauté pan or wok, rolling the oil around to coat the bottom and sides.

3. When the oil is very hot, pour half of the egg mixture in so that it coats the bottom. It should look like you're making a giant pancake.

4. Lower heat to medium-low and cook thoroughly, flipping once. Remove from pan and cut the egg into long thin strips.

5. In the same pan, add a little more oil and sauté the onion and green pepper over medium-low heat until the onion is soft and translucent.

6. Lower the heat to low and add the minced garlic. Continue to cook for about 1 to 2 minutes more. Don't let the garlic brown.

7. Add the rice and a little more oil and fry for about 5 minutes, stirring frequently. Add some chicken broth or stock, enough to flavor the rice, but not enough to make it soupy.

8. Add the rest of the scrambled eggs and a dash or two of "salsa china" (soy sauce). Add the diced lechón and stir sparingly. Continue cooking for 5 minutes.

9. Gently fold in the green onions, green peas, and egg strips. Remove from heat, cover, and let stand for a minute or two. Serve hot.

VARIATION: SEAFOOD

If you want a seafood twist, omit the lechón or ham and sauté some small shrimp, lobster tail meat, or crabmeat in a little bacon fat. Add to the rice just before serving.

Serves 4 to 6

CHINESE CUBANS

The Chinese people first came to Cuba in the 1840s. Sugar plantation owners started bringing workers in from China to shore up the workforce in the cane fields. With new attitudes and laws against slavery, the worldwide slave trade was in decline and Chinese workers were willing to work for low pay. Cutting cane is laborious work, and the conditions in the fields are very hazardous. The leaves and stalks of the cane can be very sharp and it's easy to get small cuts in the skin—cuts that don't heal quickly in the damp, tropical climate.

The Chinese that came were indentured servants—that meant that they were little better off than slaves. They had to work for a fixed period to pay off the cost of their passage from China. However, once the contract was satisfied, many Chinese headed to Havana to start small businesses and become trades people.

It has become kind of a cliché, but yes, many enterprising Chinese started restaurants and laundries. Most of the Chinese settled in the same Havana neighborhood. Soon you saw street and shop signs in both Spanish and Chinese. The citizens of Havana's Chinatown even had their own Chinese language newspapers and theaters.

Chinese people continued to immigrate to Cuba in the twentieth century. Many came because they had family in Cuba. Many more came, quite ironically, to escape communism at home. Raúl remembers buying fried fish from a Chinese street corner vendor—a common site in the 1940s and 1950s.

With Castro's revolution in 1959, many Chinese fled the island to the United States. There are still many people throughout Cuba and Cubans around the world who have some Chinese blood. In Miami, we know several Chinese Cubans—the original Chino-Latinos.

Arroz con Mariscos
Rice with Seafood

Raúl: Even where the nearest ocean is a thousand miles away, seafood is a popular choice for parties.

Jorge: You can serve a festive seafood dish that will satisfy your hungry guests without busting your budget.

Glenn: This delicious Cuban specialty combines the great taste of seafood with delicately seasoned rice. The rice helps you stretch your seafood and still present an impressive dish to your guests.

Raúl: You can make this great dish simply in an hour or less from start to finish.

Shrimp and lobster tail shells
2 quarts water
1 teaspoon salt
2 cups diced white onions
1½ cups diced red bell pepper
1½ cups diced green bell pepper
¼ cup olive oil
6 cloves garlic, crushed and finely chopped
6 cups shrimp broth (see step 1 below)
3 cups parboiled rice
1 cup chopped Roma tomatoes
1 teaspoon Bijol powder
1½ teaspoons salt

¼ teaspoon pepper
6 strips bacon, diced
1 pound large shrimp, peeled, deveined, and butterflied (reserve shells)
1 pound bay scallops
2 (4- to 6-ounce) lobster tails
½ pound fish fillets (any ocean fish will do)
Salt, pepper, and ground cumin for seasoning seafood
2 tablespoons fresh lemon juice
¼ cup flour
⅔ cup frozen green peas

1. Make a broth by placing the shells from the shrimp and lobster in a 3-quart saucepan and filling it with about 2 quarts of lightly salted water. Bring to a boil, reduce heat to low and simmer, uncovered, for about 15 minutes.

2. Sauté the onions and red and green peppers in olive oil in a large sauté pan until the onion is translucent. Add the garlic and cook an additional minute, stirring frequently.

3. Remove the simmering broth from the heat and strain out all of the shells. Take 6 cups of the seafood broth and pour into a large 8-quart covered pot.

4. Add the cooked onion mixture, rice, tomatoes, Bijol powder, salt, and pepper. Bring to a boil, reduce heat to low, cover, and simmer until rice is fully cooked and most of the liquid has been absorbed, about 30 to 45 minutes.

5. While the rice cooks, sauté the bacon in a large frying pan. Reduce heat to medium-low and let the fat render out of the bacon, about 10 minutes. Once the fat releases, remove the bacon and increase the temperature to high. Reserve bacon.

6. Sauté the shrimp, scallops and lobster tails in small batches in this hot bacon fat, starting with the peeled shrimp. You may add a little olive oil to the pan as necessary. Season each batch of seafood lightly with salt, pepper, and a little cumin. Sauté the seafood quickly, flipping once after a minute or so, until the shrimp turn pink, and the scallops and lobster turn opaque, about 3 to 5 minutes. Do not overcook.

(continued on page 128)

(continued from page 126)

7. Remove each batch of seafood from pan and set aside somewhere where it will keep warm, but not continue cooking.

8. Sprinkle a little lemon juice on the fish fillets and lightly season them with salt, pepper and a little cumin. Dredge the fillets in the flour and fry them in the pan until just cooked through.

9. Fluff the rice up with a fork. Carefully fold the peas, bacon, and the cooked seafood into the cooked rice. Cover and cook over low heat for about 3 minutes—just long enough to make sure everything is hot. Serve immediately.

Serves 6 to 8

CUBAN PARTIES: EL DÍA DE TRES REYES—THREE KINGS DAY

Glenn: Cubans assimilated many American Christmas traditions into their culture. One tradition that caused a battle in many families revolved around the jolly fat man who has become the centerpiece of the American Christmas.

Raúl: In Cuba, there was no Santa Claus.

Jorge: And not many chimneys for him either.

Glenn: Most Cuban families clung to the religious traditions of Christmas.

Jorge: In Cuba, we did not give out gifts on Christmas day. Instead, we had our gifts on the 6th of January in observation of 'Los Tres Reyes Magos, or the "The Three Magician Kings."

Glenn: What Americans call the "Three Wise Men" or just Three Kings. In this case, El Rey Melchior brings gold, El Rey Baltazar brings myrrh, and El Rey Gaspar is the one with the frankincense.

Raúl: The problems started in the early 1950s, when many "modern" Cuban families, mostly

affluent people who lived in the Miramar section of Havana, tried to bring Santa Claus into their Christmas celebrations. Cubans call him Santicló, the Cuban Santa.

Glenn: Santicló had the same trappings as the American Santa: white beard, big belly, and red clothes—wait a minute that sounds a lot like Jorge on Valentine's Day.

Jorge: Very funny.

Glenn: Anyway, old Santicló brought his presents on Christmas Eve when the children were sleeping; placing them under the American Christmas tree most people kept in their living rooms.

Raúl: Real Cubans never accepted Santa Claus. There is no Santicló in the Castillo or Musibay households.

Jorge: No, we stick with the old traditions we grew up with in Cuba. Although it has become very hard to do this in Miami, many families still wait to open their Christmas gifts on Three Kings Day.

Raúl: When I was young, Los Tres Reyes Magos

day was a very big deal. In many Cuban towns, the day was marked with a big, formal procession.

Jorge: Men dressed as the Kings would lead the parade, tossing candy and treats to the children.

Glenn: These Epiphany parades are history in Cuba. Castro banned anything even remotely religious after he took power.

Jorge: If you'd like to celebrate a true Cuban Christmas, you need to save at least one Christmas present to open on January 6. Most Christian religions celebrate the feast of the Epiphany, so you may be resurrecting one of your own family traditions.

Glenn: Traditional Three Kings Day foods include grass, straw, water . . .

Jorge: And any other food item you think may be attractive to a camel.

Raúl: The humans like to eat a good, though simple meal. This is a time for family and quiet celebration, not a big party like New Year's Eve.

Camarones con Queso
Shrimp with Cheese

¼ cup olive oil

¼ cup minced yellow onion

1½ pounds shrimp, peeled, deveined, and butterflied

3 cloves garlic, minced

1 teaspoon ground cumin

1 teaspoon sweet Spanish paprika

½ teaspoon salt

Freshly ground black pepper

Juice of ½ a lime

½ cup grated cheese (Provolone, Muenster, or Gouda—any white mild cheese)

1. Heat the olive oil in a large sauté pan. Add the onion and sauté for a minute or two over medium-high heat.

2. Add the shrimp, garlic, cumin, paprika, salt, and pepper. Continue to cook, stirring occasionally until the shrimp are completely cooked. This whole process shouldn't take more than 5 minutes, so please don't overcook. Taste one of the shrimp and adjust seasonings to taste.

3. Add the fresh lime juice and toss. Sprinkle the top of the shrimp with the cheese. Immediately cover and remove from heat.

4. Let stand for a minute or two, just long enough to melt the cheese. Serve immediately.

Serves 4

IF YOU LOCK 10 CUBANS IN A ROOM . . .

*We like to say that there are as many ways to cook Cuban food as there are Cubans in Havana. The nice thing about Cuban food is its adaptability to individual tastes and cooking styles. There is no one ultimate recipe for any dish in Cuban cuisine. In fact, the very best cooks never follow a recipe exactly; they add a little of this and a little of that. Knowing what to put in and how much to use is what makes the **art** of Cuban cooking.*

If you lock 10 Cubans in a room you'll come up with 20 different recipes—the one they came in with and the one they improvised on the spot to outdo the next guy. Cuban cooking can be very competitive!

Glenn: This recipe started in a meal we had in one of those Mexican party restaurants in Cancun. If you've been to Cancun, you know the kind of place I'm talking about. A man dressed like Pancho Villa runs around trying to get you to tip your head back so that he can pour a lot of tequila down your unsuspecting throat.

Jorge: Wow that sounds a lot like our nephew Neil's last birthday party.

Glenn: Anyway, in a place like this, we didn't expect to get a very good meal. However, a shrimp and cheese dish pleasantly surprised us.

Jorge: In the Yucatan, many of the flavors used in cooking are similar to Cuban dishes; they also use citrus and garlic marinades in many dishes.

Raúl: They also don't use the hot fiery peppers that are common in the rest of Mexico.

Glenn: Anyway, that one memorable meal in Cancun inspired this recipe.

Arroz con Salchichas
Rice with Vienna Sausages

Jorge: Many people forget the strong influence of Cuba's neighbor to the North, the United States.

Glenn: The American influence has been evident throughout Cuba's history, with the peak in the 1950s. American culture brought to Cuba cakes, and queso americano, and pan molde (American white bread), and Spam—just to name a few.

Raúl: Another popular import is the Vienna sausage, those "wieners in a can" that you have probably eaten at parties.

Glenn: The Cubans took this American favorite and gave it a delicious twist with rice. I've never been a big fan of those little cocktail wienies, but this dish takes this humble canned sausage to new heights.

2 cups chopped green bell peppers
2 cups chopped onion
¼ cup olive oil for frying (some also use lard)
4 cloves garlic, minced
4 small Roma tomatoes, chopped
4 cups parboiled rice
3 cups ham broth (see "stock" in the glossary)
1 cup tomato sauce
1 cup white wine
1 teaspoon salt
3 (9-ounce) cans Vienna sausage links
½ teaspoon Bijol powder
½ cup whole pitted green olives
½ cup whole pitted black olives

1. Sauté the green peppers and onion in olive oil or lard until limp. Add the garlic and sauté an additional minute or two. Add the chopped tomatoes and let simmer for about 5 minutes.

2. Place this vegetable mixture into a large covered saucepan. Add rice, ham broth, tomato sauce, wine, salt, sausage links, and Bijol powder. For an added kick, stir in green and black olives.

3. Bring to a boil, reduce heat to low, cover, and let simmer until the rice is cooked, approximately 20 to 30 minutes.

Serves 6

Bistec Encebollado
Steak with Onions

Glenn: A nice beef steak, perfectly prepared and nicely presented, is a great choice for a dinner party.

Raúl: This recipe adds a touch of lime and fresh cilantro to give the dish a Cuban flavor.

Jorge: We've had great luck using sweet onions, such as the Vidalia onion. However, feel free to use whatever onion you have on hand.

Raúl: Cubans traditionally eat their beef steaks thin.

Glenn: Every meat market and grocery store in Miami has special thin cuts, such as the churrasco, that cater to the Cuban taste. You can also use a good sirloin to make this recipe.

2 pounds sirloin steak, sliced thin (about 8 ounces per serving)
¼ cup olive oil for sautéing
2 cups thinly sliced sweet onions
2 cups sliced fresh mushrooms (optional)
1 teaspoon salt
½ teaspoon black pepper
½ teaspoon cumin
½ teaspoon sweet Spanish paprika
6 cloves garlic, minced
2 tablespoons fresh lime juice
4 tablespoons butter
Chopped fresh cilantro

1. Using a meat mallet, moisten the steaks with a little water and place between two pieces of plastic wrap and pound out to a thickness of about 1/4 inch.

2. Heat the olive oil in a frying pan over medium heat. Add the onions and sauté briefly. They should still be slightly crisp. Remove onions. (If you are using mushrooms, add them and remove at the same time as the onions.)

3. Sprinkle each steak with salt, black pepper, cumin, and paprika and rub it in.

4. Add the garlic to the pan and sauté for 1 minute only. Immediately add the steaks and sauté to desired doneness, turning once only. These thin steaks will cook very quickly. Medium-rare calls for a very quick flip—no more than a minute or so on each side.

5. Remove the steaks and place them somewhere where they'll stay warm and away from the grasping mitts of your hungry sister-in-law. Deglaze the pan by adding the lime juice and the butter and continuing to heat, stirring constantly. Cook long enough to reduce (thicken) somewhat.

6. Cover each steak with the sautéed onions and mushrooms. Pour the sauce over the steaks and sprinkle with chopped cilantro.

Serves 4

Camarones en Crema con Cilantro
Shrimp in Cilantro Cream Sauce

Glenn: You may think of cilantro only as the herb that gives so many tomato-based dishes their bite.

Jorge: It's amazing that the combination of cilantro and cream creates a very subtle yet rich flavor, you might even say it's sublime.

Raúl: I wouldn't say that because I'm not sure what kind of a lime you're talking about!

Glenn: Despite its complete lack of lime, this recipe creates an elegant dish with a smooth and unique taste.

2 pounds shrimp, peeled and deveined (shells reserved)
1 quart lightly salted water (to make shrimp stock)
½ cup (1 stick) salted butter
¼ cup flour
1 cup shrimp stock (see step 1 below)
¼ cup white wine
½ cup chopped onion
¼ cup olive oil
1 cup seeded and chopped Roma tomatoes
4 cloves garlic, chopped
Salt and pepper to taste
1 cup heavy cream
⅓ cup chopped fresh cilantro

1. Make a stock by boiling the shells of the shrimp in lightly salted water. Strain and reserve the stock.

2. Make the sauce first. Use a 3-quart saucepan and melt the butter over medium-low heat until it just begins to brown.

3. Whisk in the flour quickly to make a smooth roux or paste.

4. Add 1 cup shrimp stock and the wine, blending with your whisk to avoid any lumps. Simmer over low heat, stirring constantly until the sauce thickens. Remove from direct heat, but cover and keep warm for later.

5. Sauté the onion in the olive oil in a large sauté pan over medium heat, until it begins to soften.

6. Add the shrimp and continue to sauté for a minute or two only, flipping frequently.

7. Add the tomatoes and the garlic and cook for an additional 3 to 5 minutes, stirring occasionally. Salt and pepper to taste.

8. While the shrimp is cooking, finish your sauce. Add the cream with a whisk and blend in thoroughly. Increase heat to medium to bring the sauce up to serving temperature. Stir constantly and do not let the sauce come to a boil.

9. Remove sauce from heat and add the cilantro. Pour the sauce over the shrimp and vegetables in the sauté pan, turning with a spoon to blend.

10. Serve immediately over white rice.

Serves 4 to 6

Camarones para una Boda Cubana
Cuban Wedding Shrimp

Glenn: **This is a recipe for the best dish we ever had at an otherwise mediocre pseudo-Cuban restaurant.**

Jorge: **They called this recipe "Cuban Wedding Shrimp."**

Raúl: **The problem is, none of us has ever heard of Cuban Wedding Shrimp.**

Jorge: **They never served any shrimp like this at any wedding I ever attended.**

Raúl: **They never served any shrimp, period!**

Glenn: **So it was back to the Three Guys kitchens to try to duplicate what we have to admit is a very tasty appetizer.**

Jorge: **Believe us, ours is a lot better—even if it isn't any more authentic.**

SAUCE
½ cup dark rum
½ cup orange juice
¼ cup white vinegar

¼ cup brown sugar
¾ teaspoon salt

SHRIMP
½ cup slivered onion
½ cup slivered green bell pepper
Olive oil (about 4 tablespoons)
16 large shrimp, peeled, deveined, and butterflied

2 cloves garlic, finely chopped
Salt
Red pepper flakes

1. In a small bowl, whisk together the rum, orange juice, vinegar, brown sugar, and salt. Set aside.
2. In a large sauté pan with a tight fitting lid, sauté the onion and green pepper in the olive oil for just a minute or two over medium-high heat.
3. Toss in the shrimp and the garlic and fry for 2 minutes longer, no more no less, turning frequently.
4. Add the mixed liquids, cover the pan tightly, and remove from heat. Let stand for 5 minutes, away from heat, covered tightly. No peeking and we mean no peeking!
5. Remove the shrimp and vegetables from the pan and refrigerate, covered, until well chilled.
6. Reserve liquid in the pan and bring to a rapid boil under high heat. Stirring occasionally, boil the sauce until it reduces by half. The sauce should be thicker than water, but not syrupy.
7. Run the sauce through a strainer and refrigerate until completely chilled.
8. Serve cold by plating individual servings—4 shrimp on a bed of onions and green peppers.
9. Ladle some of the chilled sauce on top of the shrimp and vegetables on each plate, just enough to make a small pool. Sprinkle each plate with a pinch of salt (trust us on this one) and some red pepper flakes—just enough to give it a little color.

Serves 4

CUBAN WEDDINGS

If you go to a Cuban wedding in Miami, you may be surprised by how much it resembles an American wedding. Many of the traditions are the same. One tradition from Cuba is this: a Cuban bride does not toss out the bouquet to the unmarried girls at the party.

Instead, the traditional Cuban wedding cake includes something extra. The baker imbeds ribbons in the bottom layer of the cake so the ends hang out of the finished cake. A simple gold ring is attached to the end of one ribbon. Before cutting the cake, the bride gathers all of the unmar-ried girls at the wedding around the cake and each girl then pulls a ribbon from the cake.

Tradition has it that the girl who pulls the ribbon with the ring on the end is the next one to get married.

Chicharrones de Pollo
Chicken Pieces

Glenn: Chicharrones de Pollo are small pieces of chicken, marinated for a couple of hours with a citrus marinade, coated with flour, and fried.

Jorge: They are kind of like a Cuban version of those fast food chicken nuggets—only get this, we make ours with real chicken!

Glenn: Serve them with rice and frijoles or a side of yuca and you have a delicious dinner.

Jorge: Do not over-marinate this dish. The high acid content will pickle the chicken.

6 cloves garlic, mashed
1 medium onion, chopped
1 cup fresh lime juice
½ cup light rum
1½ pounds boneless, skinless chicken
   thighs, cut in strips
Salt
Pepper

Cumin
Oregano, ground
Vegetable oil for frying
1 cup flour
2 teaspoons salt
2 teaspoons black pepper
1 egg beaten with 2 tablespoons water

1. Make a marinade with the garlic, onion, lime juice, and rum.

2. Arrange the chicken pieces in a shallow glass baking pan. Pour the marinade over the chicken pieces and mix them up so that all of the pieces are well coated. Cover with plastic wrap and refrigerate for about 2 to 3 hours.

3. After marinating, season the chicken pieces on the top layer by eye with salt, pepper, cumin, and oregano.

   TIP: Use a mortar and pestle to finely grind the oregano.

4. Heat vegetable oil in a large skillet, deep enough to cover half the thickness of the chicken at one time.

5. Mix the flour with the salt and pepper and place in a shallow pan. Make an egg wash by beating a whole egg with a little water.

6. Remove the chicken pieces from the marinade (shaking off some of the excess marinade), dip each piece in the egg wash, and dredge in the seasoned flour mixture. (As you work down a layer, re-season the newly exposed layer with more salt, pepper, oregano, and cumin.)

7. Fry the chicken pieces, in small batches—don't crowd the pan—until all sides are golden brown and the chicken is completely cooked through.

8. Serve with rice or another side dish.

Serves 4

Chuletas de Puerco
Pork Chops

Glenn: There is nothing like a good pork chop.

Raúl: In Cuba, we enjoyed pork chops in the Cuban style with plenty of garlic, cumin, and sour orange.

Jorge: A thin-cut chop works best—it allows more of the marinade and spices to infuse the meat and give it a great flavor.

1 teaspoon dried oregano
¼ teaspoon ground cumin
5 cloves garlic
½ teaspoon black peppercorns
1 teaspoon salt
6 pork chops
¼ cup orange juice
¼ cup vinegar
¼ cup olive oil

2 large onions, sliced
1 cup tomato sauce
½ cup red wine
Flour for dusting
Olive oil for frying
Avocado slices
Salt and pepper to taste
Fresh lime juice

1. Use a mortar and pestle to crush the oregano and cumin. Add the garlic, peppercorns, and salt to the mortar and crush until you have a smooth paste. Generously smear the chops with this paste. Place the chops in a glass baking dish.

2. Whisk the orange juice, vinegar, and olive oil together in a small mixing bowl. Cover the pork chops with the sliced onions and the orange juice mixture. Seal the baking pan with plastic wrap and refrigerate for a minimum of 4 hours.

3. Remove the pork chops from the marinade. Pat them dry with paper towels. Place the marinade and the onions in a 2-quart saucepan with the tomato sauce and wine. Bring to a boil, then reduce heat to low, and let simmer, uncovered, stirring occasionally.

4. Meanwhile, lightly dust the pork chops on both sides with flour. Heat some olive oil in a large sauté pan until it just begins to smoke. Quickly add the pork chops and brown on both sides. Reduce heat to medium low and continue to fry the chops until they are cooked through, about 12 to 14 minutes.

5. Serve the chops with plenty of sauce poured over the top. Garnish with slices of fresh avocado seasoned with salt, pepper, and lime juice.

Serves 6

Filete Bistec Salteado
Cuban Beef Stir-Fry

Jorge: Cuban steaks are usually sliced very thin and either cooked very quickly, or slow cooked with plenty of liquid.

Glenn: One exception is Filete Bistec Salteado, a type of Cuban stir-fry that is popular at many Cuban restaurants.

Jorge: This recipe is our take on this famous dish. You cut good quality beef tenderloin filets into thick chunks.

Raúl: The deep-fat fried potatoes are the key ingredient, making this a true "meat and potatoes" dish.

Vegetable oil for deep-fat frying
2 cups diced potatoes
1½ cups chopped onion
1½ cups chopped green bell pepper
1 cup sliced Spanish chorizo
1 cup sliced fresh mushrooms
6 cloves garlic, chopped
½ teaspoon salt
½ teaspoon pepper

½ teaspoon cumin
2 tablespoons flour
¼ cup red wine
2 pounds beef tenderloin filet, cut in strips
Salt, pepper, and cumin for seasoning meat
Flour for dredging
Olive oil for frying

1. Heat about 2 inches of vegetable oil (enough to cover the potatoes) in a frying pan to 350 degrees F. (You may also use a deep fryer if you have one.) Fry the potatoes in the hot oil, turning occasionally until golden brown on all sides.

2. Remove potatoes from oil, drain, and keep hot.

3. Sauté the onion and green peppers in a large frying pan for about 3 minutes. Toss in the chorizos and mushrooms, garlic, salt, pepper, and cumin and cook another minute or two.

4. Stir in flour, add the wine, and let cook an additional 5 minutes, stirring frequently.

5. Remove everything that you have now collected in the pan and set aside where it will stay hot. The flour should help thicken the sauce slightly.

6. Season the tenderloin strips with salt, pepper, and cumin by eye. Dredge the strips in the flour, shaking off any excess.

7. Add a little more oil to the pan and fry the tenderloin in hot olive oil just long enough to cook to the desired doneness, turning frequently. Just a few minutes for rare beef.

8. Add everything else you've cooked up to this point, tossing to mix completely.

9. Quickly toss the hot-fried potatoes into the mix and serve immediately.

Serves 4

Fricasé de Pollo
Chicken Fricassee

Jorge: The fricassee is a classic of French cooking.

Glenn: It is also a Cuban favorite. We can only guess that the French influence brought this dish to Cuba, most likely through Haiti. In the 1800s, many French refugees of the Haitian revolution arrived in Santiago de Cuba and Baracoa from Haiti.

Raúl: Many of these people went on to own large coffee plantations in Cuba.

Jorge: The Cuban influence on this dish is apparent in the use of sour orange juice and lots of garlic.

Raúl: Another thing that makes this dish unique, you remove the skin from the chicken before cooking in a very traditional Cuban style.

½ cup sour orange juice (or use sour orange substitute)
6 cloves garlic, peeled and minced
1½ teaspoons salt
½ teaspoon fresh ground black pepper
4 pounds chicken pieces, skinned
¼ cup flour for dusting chicken pieces
⅓ cup olive oil

1 cup red potatoes, peeled and cubed
2 cups chopped onions
1 cup chopped green bell pepper
1 cup tomato sauce
1 cup wine
½ cup stuffed green olives
½ cup raisins

1. Use a large non-metallic bowl and whisk together the sour orange juice, garlic, salt, and pepper.
2. Add the chicken pieces to the marinade, cover, and refrigerate a minimum of 4 hours, but preferably overnight.
3. Remove the chicken from the marinade and blot on paper towels to dry. Reserve marinade.
4. Use a large covered frying pan. Lightly season the chicken pieces with salt, pepper, and cumin and dust with flour. Heat the olive oil in the pan until it just starts to smoke.
5. Quickly (and carefully) add the chicken pieces to the hot oil, browning on both sides, just a minute or two per side. Do this in two small batches. Remove chicken and set aside.
6. Sauté the potato cubes in the same hot oil until lightly browned on all sides. Remove potatoes and set aside.
7. Sauté the onions and green pepper until limp. Return the chicken to the pan. Add the reserved marinade, tomato sauce, wine, olives, raisins, and browned potatoes.
8. Cover, reduce heat to low, and simmer until the chicken is done, about 20 to 30 minutes. Don't overcook. Serve the chicken pieces over white rice with plenty of sauce.

Serves 4

SOUR ORANGE JUICE—THE REAL THING AND THE SUBSTITUTE

Whenever a recipe calls for sour orange juice, the orange juice in question is naranja agria or bitter orange. If you can't get sour orange juice in your area, you can make this substitution in all recipes:

Two parts orange juice

One part lemon juice

One part lime juice

This is about as close as you can get to the real thing. You may also order bottled sour orange juice from several companies. See the "Sources" section for complete details.

Guiso de Maíz
Corn Stew

Jorge: Guiso de Maíz is the dish your grandmother might have made for you in Cuba.

Raúl: It is a simple, country dish—very down to earth.

Glenn: In Cuba, guiso was the dish to make when the corn came in.

Jorge: Maíz criollo (country corn) is the most common type of corn in Cuba. It's closer in flavor and texture to field corn in the United States.

Raúl: To use in cooking, you have to pick the corn when it is still quite young— what's called the milk stage. If you don't pick it soon enough, it becomes hard and tough—that's when you feed it to the pigs.

Glenn: In the United States, fresh sweet corn is the best choice for this dish.

Raúl: If you can't find any in the off season, those whole frozen ears in the freezer section of your local super-market will do in a pinch.

Glenn: Did someone say whole frozen ears?

Jorge: That pretty much describes Glenn in the middle of a Minnesota winter!

½ pound tasajo
½ pound salt pork
4 ears fresh sweet corn, cut in 1-inch wheels
4 ears fresh sweet corn, kernels cut from the cob
2 ears fresh sweet corn, kernels cut from the cob and ground with ½ teaspoon of salt
1 cup cubed white potato
¼ cup masa harina or white all-purpose flour
1 cup chopped onion
½ cup chopped green bell pepper

Olive oil for sautéing
3 cloves garlic
½ cup tomato sauce
¼ cup white wine
1 teaspoon vinegar
½ pound ham, chunked
½ pound Spanish chorizo, sliced
1 teaspoon salt
¼ teaspoon black pepper
½ teaspoon cumin
6 cups chicken stock or broth
1 cup calabaza, cut up (may substitute butternut squash)

1. Get a nice chunk of tasajo—dried beef that you'll find in many Latin markets. Remove the fat layer from the tasajo, place it in a saucepan and cover with cold fresh water. Bring to a boil, then reduce heat to low and let simmer for 30 minutes. Drain.

2. Cover the tasajo again with cold fresh water. Bring to a boil, then reduce heat to low and let simmer for 45 minutes to 1 hour, until the meat is tender. Drain and let cool.

3. Cut the salt pork into bite-size chunks.

4. Husk all of the corn and peel the potatoes. Take 4 ears corn and cut them into ruedas or wheels about 2 inches thick.

5. Take 4 more ears corn and use a sharp knife to remove the corn kernels from the cobs. Set aside. Do the same thing with your last 2 ears of corn. Place these corn kernels in a food processor and grind together with ½ teaspoon salt and either masa harina or flour. Add just enough masa or flour until you have a moldable dough. Set aside.

6. Use a large, 8-quart covered stockpot. Sauté the onion and green pepper in the olive oil until tender.

7. Add the garlic, the salt pork, and the tasajo and sauté another minute or two stirring constantly.

8. Add the tomato sauce, wine, vinegar, ham, chorizo, salt, pepper, cumin, and chicken stock. Bring the stew to a boil, reduce heat to low, and let simmer. Cook for about 5 minutes, stirring occasionally.

(continued on page 148)

(continued from page 146)

9. Add all of the vegetables to the stew except the ground corn mixture. Bring the stew to a rolling boil, then reduce heat until you have a slow simmer.

10. Carefully drop the ground corn/masa mixture by packed teaspoonfuls into the hot stew. This will make little corn dumplings.

11. Don't stir, touch, molest, or even look sideways at the stew for the next 10 minutes. This will allow the dumplings to achieve a state of permanent togetherness. Finally, reduce heat to low, cover and simmer for about 20 to 30 minutes.

12. Adjust seasonings and serve hot.

Serves 6

Frita de Pollo
Fried Shredded Chicken

Olive oil
1 large onion, sliced in large chunks
1 carrot, sliced in large chunks
1 celery stalk, sliced in large chunks
12 bone-in, skin-on chicken thighs
1 bay leaf
½ teaspoon salt
Olive oil for sautéing

2½ cups thinly sliced yellow onion
6 cloves garlic, chopped
1½ teaspoons cumin
¼ cup lime juice
½ cup white wine
4 tablespoons butter
1 tablespoon minced fresh cilantro
Salt and pepper to taste

1. Use an 8-quart or larger stockpot. Heat a little olive oil in the bottom of the pan over high heat until it starts to smoke, then quickly add the onion, carrot, and celery. Stir and toss constantly to get all of the vegetables covered with oil and starting to brown slightly, about 3 or 4 minutes. Add the chicken, bay leaf, and salt to the stockpot. Add enough water to the pot to cover all of the ingredients.

2. Bring the water to a boil, reduce heat to low and simmer, uncovered, until the chicken is cooked through and tender, about 1 hour.

3. Remove the chicken pieces from the pan and set aside to let cool.

4. Run the broth in the pan through a strainer. You now have a delicious chicken stock that you can use in other recipes. The stock will keep in the refrigerator for several days. You may also freeze the stock—many people use an ice cube tray to freeze it in small cubes, for later use.

5. Skin and de-bone the chicken. Use a fork to shred the chicken, it should be very tender.

6. Cover the bottom of a large sauté pan with olive oil and heat until it just begins to smoke. Toss in the thinly sliced onions and chicken, reduce heat immediately to medium-high, and fry, stirring constantly until the onions get limp and the chicken browns slightly. Add the garlic and cumin and sauté just a minute longer, stirring constantly.

7. Remove everything from the pan and keep warm.

8. Return the pan to the stovetop and deglaze it with the lime juice and wine. *TIP: Juice your lime before you start sautéing the chicken. You need to be quick when you deglaze the pan.)*

9. Use a spoon to stir up all of the "crispy critters" from the bottom of the pan. Let the juices come to a boil and continue boiling until you reduce the juices by about half. Finally, add the butter and the cilantro.

10. Return the chicken and onions to the pan and toss with the sauce. Season with a little salt and pepper to taste. Garnish with a sprig or two of cilantro.

Serves 4

Glenn: Vaca frita has always been a very popular Cuban dish. Tender, slow-cooked beef is shredded and then fried with onions and spices.

Raúl: Cuba once boasted one of the highest rates of per capita consumption of beef in the Caribbean.

Jorge: However, in the 1960s and beyond, beef became very rare in Cuba. That's because the government declared that only the state could slaughter cattle and sell the meat. A farmer who killed a cow could face a long prison sentence.

Glenn: Years of neglect and mismanagement also decimated the cattle population in Cuba.

Raúl: The only way to get beef was if a car or truck hit a cow. If you happened to be in an area where one of these unfortunate accidents occurred, you might be able to buy some beef from the owner of the "unlucky" cow.

Glenn: This dish actually pre-dates the lack of beef in Cuba. Many Cuban families enjoyed this variation made with tender chicken. On some menus, you'll see this called either vaca frita de pollo or carne frita de pollo.

Langosta a la Cubana
Cuban Style Lobster

Jorge: In Miami, we eat many spiny lobsters, which are abundant in the coastal waters off Florida.

Glenn: The spiny lobster is a warm-water lobster, and unlike its Maine cousin, it doesn't have any claws.

Raúl: I also believe that the spiny lobster has a much sweeter flavor.

Jorge: When most Americans think lobster, they think of a whole lobster with plenty of melted butter.

Raúl: You don't see many people eating lobster that way in Miami! We like to give our lobster a Cuban touch with sofrito and the salty bite of a good Spanish chorizo.

¼ cup olive oil
1 cup finely chopped onion
1 cup finely chopped green bell pepper
5 cloves garlic, finely chopped
2 cups peeled and chopped fresh Roma tomatoes
½ cup white wine
½ cup chicken broth or fish stock

2 tablespoons tomato paste
½ cup sliced Spanish chorizo links, casings removed
6 lobster tails, shell removed and cut in fifths
1 teaspoon cumin
Salt and pepper to taste
½ cup chopped cilantro

1. Make a sofrito by adding olive oil to a large sauté pan and sautéing the chopped onion and green pepper. After the onion begins to soften, add the garlic and tomatoes and sauté another minute or two, stirring constantly.

2. Add the wine, stock, and tomato paste; reduce heat to low and let simmer, uncovered, for about 15 minutes, stirring occasionally.

3. Add a little oil to another sauté pan and sauté the chorizo over medium heat, stirring occasionally. Remove and reserve chorizo.

4. Increase heat slightly and when the oil starts to sizzle, toss in the lobster chunks and quickly stir-fry, flipping and turning constantly. Add cumin, a dash of salt, and some fresh ground pepper. Do not overcook.

5. Now, dump the lobster and any oil that remains in the pan into the by now bubbling sofrito. Toss in your chorizo and the cilantro. Turn just a few times with a spoon to blend, and immediately remove from heat.

6. Serve hot over rice.

Serves 4

Pavo Asado Relleno a la Glenn
Glenn's Stuffed Roasted Turkey

Jorge: **Probably the most popular "Cubanized" version of roast turkey in Miami is the one stuffed with moros y cristianos.**

Glenn: **I have eaten that Cubanized type of turkey several times and I do like it. However, I grew up eating turkey with a bread-based stuffing. For me, there is nothing like it. I remember when I was young and I would come downstairs in my pajamas early on Thanksgiving morning to the delightful smell of celery, onions, and pork sausage frying in the pan.**

Raúl: **Those smells were only possible because Glenn's mom was up even earlier.**

Glenn: **So I decided to create my own "Cubanized" turkey with a delicious Latin-spiced stuffing.**

Jorge: **The key to this recipe is to use unseasoned bread strips or cubes. Otherwise, the subtle Cuban spices will be overwhelmed.**

1 cup lime juice
8 cloves garlic
1 teaspoon salt
½ teaspoon ground black pepper

2 teaspoons oregano
2 teaspoons ground cumin
1 cup olive oil
1 (12- to 14- pound) turkey, fresh or frozen

STUFFING
2 pounds fresh ground pork
3 strips bacon, finely chopped
4 cloves garlic
10 black peppercorns
1 teaspoon oregano
1½ teaspoons salt
2 teaspoons cumin
1 tablespoon sweet Spanish paprika
¼ cup vinegar

¼ cup olive oil
1½ cups chopped celery
1 cup chopped onion
1 cup chopped green bell pepper
4 cloves garlic, chopped
½ teaspoon cumin
12 cups dried bread, stripped or cubed
    (or use unseasoned croutons)
4 cups turkey stock (see next page)

TURKEY SEASONING
Salt
Pepper
Cumin

Oregano
Turkey stock (see next page)

GRAVY
2 to 3 tablespoons white flour
1 cup whole milk, at room temperature
   (more or less)

Salt and pepper to taste

THE NIGHT BEFORE

1. Use a blender. Add the lime juice and garlic and process until you obliterate the garlic—we're talking total garlic annihilation.

2. Add the dry spices and blend at low speed.

3. Finally, add the olive oil and blend briefly at high speed to emulsify.

4. Make sure you have a good quality turkey sized according to the number of people you expect to serve. A 12- to 14-pound turkey roasts great and provides plenty of room for the stuffing. It also ensures that your guests are appropriately stuffed.

5. If you start with a frozen turkey, make sure to thaw it completely using the instructions on the label. If you need a larger bird to accommodate your large group, adjust the recipe ingredients proportionally.

6. Remove all of the insides from the turkey—your turkey supplier has usually made this easy for you by putting everything in a little paper bag. Place the heart, gizzard, neck, etc., in a plastic bag and store it in the refrigerator. You'll need it tomorrow.

7. Rinse the turkey inside and out with cold water and lightly pat the skin dry.

8. Place the turkey in a very large plastic bag. We use a clean white kitchen trash bag. It's important to keep the marinade away from any metallic surface—like your turkey roasting pan.

9. Pour half of the prepared marinade into the body cavity of the turkey. Add the rest of the marinade to the bag; remove excess air by squeezing the bag and seal. (This will ensure that the marinade makes good contact with the outside of your bird.)

10. Place the turkey in the refrigerator—we usually place it in the bottom of the turkey roaster in case the bag leaks—and marinate overnight.

THANKSGIVING MORNING

At home Glenn gets up early and spends most of the morning in his pajamas watching cartoons—hey, old traditions die hard. Once that's out of his system, it's on to the kitchen.

TO MAKE STOCK

1. Take the inside stuff—heart, gizzards, neck, liver and other assorted pieces you'd normally find on the inside of a turkey—and place in a 3-quart saucepan.

2. Cover with about 2 quarts lightly salted water. Bring to a boil, reduce heat to low, and simmer, uncovered, for about 45 minutes to 1 hour.

(continued on page 154)

(continued from page 153)

TO MAKE STUFFING

1. First, wash your hands thoroughly, because you're going to be using them a lot.

2. Make a sausage by mixing the ground pork with the bacon in a large bowl. You may also do this with a food processor with the metal blade, but don't overprocess.

3. Use a mortar and pestle to mash the garlic with the peppercorns and oregano. Make sure that you completely pulverize all of the peppercorns.

4. Add the mashed garlic, salt, cumin, paprika, and vinegar to the meat. Mix thoroughly, squeezing the mixture between your fingers until completely blended.

5. Now heat a little olive oil in a large sauté pan. Drop the sausage into the pan in small teaspoon-size balls.

6. Brown the sausage completely on all sides over moderate heat, stirring frequently. Use a slotted spoon to remove the cooked sausage to a large bowl.

7. Add the olive oil to the pan and when the oil is hot, add the celery, onion, and green pepper. Sauté the vegetables until the onion is translucent.

8. Add the garlic and sauté a minute longer, stirring constantly.

9. Finally, stir in the cumin. Add the vegetables and the oil from the pan to the bowl with the sausage.

10. Add dried bread strips, cubes, or croutons to the bowl. We like to make our own by slicing bread in ½-inch-thick rounds and then slicing each round into strips. Place the strips on a baking sheet and place in an oven heated to 220 degrees F for about 20 to 30 minutes.

11. If you do buy prepared bread, make sure that is unseasoned. Do not use any seasoned croutons or stuffing mixes. Many grocery stores sell dry bread strips or cubes in the bakery department—not in the aisle with the stuffing mixes.

12. Mix everything up in the bowl and gradually add 4 cups of the turkey stock until you have a very moist mixture. Yes, this is the same stock you made with those mystery turkey parts. It should have been simmering away on the back of your stove while you were working on the stuffing.

(continued on page 156)

(continued from page 154)

ROASTING THE TURKEY

1. Preheat the oven to 325 degrees F.

2. Remove the turkey from the marinade and put it in a large, heavy roasting pan, breast side up. If you have a pan with a rack, great. Use it. Pat dry with paper towels.

3. Drizzle some olive oil on the outside of the bird and generously sprinkle the turkey inside and out with salt, pepper, cumin, and oregano.

4. Loosely stuff the large cavity of the bird with stuffing. Do not overstuff the bird. It is better to leave a little airspace in the cavity. It is not necessary to "sew up the bird." The exposed stuffing will brown with the turkey, creating a golden layer of little crunchy bits that stuffing connoisseurs consider a delicacy.

5. Place any remaining stuffing in a lightly buttered casserole dish. Cover with aluminum foil and refrigerate. Bake the extra stuffing by placing the covered dish in the oven during the last hour of baking. Place a big Post-It® note on someone's forehead to remind you to take that extra stuffing out of the refrigerator when the time comes.

6. To prevent the white meat from overcooking, tightly cover the breast and wings only with aluminum foil. *Leave the foil on for most of the time in the oven, removing only during the last hour or so of roasting.*

7. Add a little turkey stock to the bottom of the roasting pan.

8. Place the stuffed turkey in the preheated oven and roast. Baste the turkey legs with the pan drippings every 20 to 30 minutes. If you run low on pan drippings, add more broth. Don't forget to remove the foil during the last hour, which will allow the skin to brown and allow you to baste the whole turkey.

9. Use a meat thermometer to check for doneness. Do not rely on that little pop-up button. Check the temperature in the thigh of the bird. The temperature must reach a minimum of 175 degrees F in the thigh before removing from the oven. A 14-pound turkey will take approximately 3½ to 4 hours.

10. Once removed from the oven, immediately cover with a tent of aluminum foil and let stand for 20 minutes before removing the stuffing and carving the bird.

11. For safety's sake, be sure to wash everything that has been exposed to raw turkey—including your hands, utensils, the sink, and anything else—with hot, soapy water. Make sure that you prepare all stuffing ingredients on a clean cutting board that has not been cross-contaminated by any raw turkey.

To make Gravy

1. You can make delicious gravy from the pan drippings. Place the roasting pan over two stove burners and bring the drippings to a boil. Gradually whisk in a few tablespoons of flour until you have a thick roux.

2. Add whole milk, a little at a time, whisking constantly, until you have a nice smooth gravy. Season to taste with salt and pepper.

NOTE: Yes, this is a long and complicated recipe. However, this is a true holiday treat and something you'll probably only make once a year. So get in the spirit of the season and have at it! Make it a family production with everyone helping in the kitchen. If this is impossible and you are stuck going it alone, we'd like to suggest that now is a good time for you to work on that "tree falling in the forest" question.

Serves about 12 to 14 (if you include plenty of side dishes)

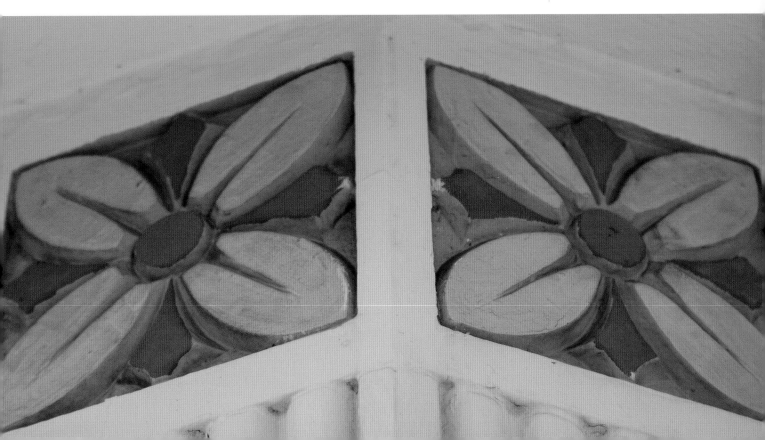

CUBAN PARTIES: DIA DE ACCIÓN DE GRACIAS—THANKSGIVING

Raúl: Of course, everyone knows the story of the first Cuban Thanksgiving.

Glenn: It all began when the Spanish Pilgrims (led by Christopher Columbus) landed at Plymouth Rock in Cuba's Oriente province.

Jorge: The pilgrims met with the native Taino Indians that first Thanksgiving Day in Cuba, and together they had a great feast.

Raúl: The Spanish pilgrims weren't very good guests. They had this crazy idea that the Tainos were hoarding a lot of gold, and they wanted it.

Glenn: What followed wasn't much of a celebration—just several years of enforced slavery, bloody battles, and death by disease. In a few short years, they wiped out most of the Taino.

Raúl: The Taino didn't have any gold! In fact, they were the original peasant farmers of Cuba.

Jorge: You can see why we never celebrated Thanksgiving in Cuba. What was there to be thankful about?

Glenn: One thing that everyone can be thankful for is the many gifts of food the Taino brought to the Cuban table.

Jorge: Probably number one in the hearts of Cubans is the yuca plant. The Taino made it into a type of bread. It took the Cubans to figure out it tasted a lot better with garlic and olive oil.

Raúl: The Taino also grew corn, bell peppers, garlic, potatoes, beans, squash, mamey, guava, boniato (a type of sweet potato), and peanuts.

Glenn: All essential ingredients in Cuban cuisine.

Raúl: The Taino were also masters of the barbecue, a word that is adapted directly from the Taino word barbacoa.

Glenn: So how about the Cuban Thanksgiving?

Jorge: Thanksgiving began for us not when the pilgrims landed at Plymouth Rock, but when the Musibays and Castillos landed in Miami.

Raúl: We never knew anything about Thanksgiving in Cuba. The only Plymouth I ever heard of was the 1956 model sedan my cousin drove!

Jorge: We were surprised to discover that everybody in America got a day off at the end of November.

Raúl: Not only that, Thanksgiving is a day when everybody eats a lot of food.

Jorge: Of course, that is just the kind of holiday celebration that Cubans can relate to.

Raúl: Cuban-Americans celebrate Thanksgiving just like all Americans do.

Jorge: Families gather to eat turkey and have a big feast. Diets go out the window as dedicated chefs compete to lay out the largest spread of holiday treats.

Glenn: Like most holidays, the Cuban exiles in America have done a few things to "Cubanize" the celebration, bringing their own foods and cooking styles to the Thanksgiving table.

Raúl: I don't think we can end this discussion without mentioning one of the great chieftains of the Taino, Hatuey.

Jorge: Hatuey was a Taino Indian cacique, or chief, who led several rebellions against the Spanish in the early sixteenth century.

Glenn: To this day, Hatuey is a hero of the Cuban people because he was one of the first to lead a rebellion against the Spanish government.

Raúl: We love Hatuey so much; we even named a beer after him.

Glenn: You'll see the signs for Hatuey Beer— pronounced "ah-tway"—all over Miami. Just look for the Indian head logo.

Jorge: The Bacardi Rum Company began brewing this beer at their Santiago Brewery in 1926.

Glenn: It's a very Cuban tradition to share this beer with a good friend. You step up to the bar and order: "un indio y dos canoas." This means, "One Indian and two canoes." You'll get a cold bottle of Hatuey and two glasses to share.

Jorge: This is a real display of friendship.

Raúl: Hey, you don't have to stop there. You can order several rounds this way to quench everyone's thirst.

Glenn: Raúl, why do I get the idea that the only reason you needed to mention Hatuey here is an excuse to go out and have a beer?

Raúl: Guilty as charged.

Jorge: Make that tres indios y tres canoas!

Pavo Relleno con Moros
Cuban Stuffed Turkey

Jorge: In Miami, a "Cubanized" version of the traditional American turkey is very popular.

Raúl: Just like many of the favorites, everybody has their own special recipe for this dish.

Jorge: We use this one at home.

Glenn: The secret to a great turkey? Start with a good, premium brand turkey.

Raúl: If you can get a fresh turkey from your butcher, great.

Jorge: Obviously, you need to completely thaw a frozen turkey (following package directions) before you begin this recipe.

Glenn: You can increase the amount of marinade and stuffing to handle just about any size bird.

MARINADE

1 (12- to 14-pound) turkey
8 cloves garlic, mashed with 1 teaspoon salt
1 tablespoon ground cumin
½ teaspoon black pepper
1 teaspoon ground oregano

½ cup sour orange juice (or substitute ⅓ cup sweet orange juice with 1 tablespoon white vinegar added)
½ cup olive oil
1 cup chopped white onion

2 cups dried black beans
4 cups water
3 cups parboiled rice
6 strips bacon, chopped
2½ cups diced white onion
2½ cups chopped green bell peppers
¼ cup olive oil for sautéing
4 cloves garlic, crushed and chopped
¼ cup tomato paste
1½ teaspoons oregano
2 teaspoons ground cumin

1 bay leaf
3 tablespoons white vinegar
5 cups turkey stock (see step 1 below)
1 teaspoon salt
½ teaspoon pepper
½ pound thick-sliced bacon
½ cup white wine

1. Remove the neck and giblet packets from the turkey. You may use these to make your own turkey stock: place in a 3-quart saucepan. Cover with about 2 quarts lightly salted water. Bring to a boil, reduce heat to low, and simmer, uncovered, for about 45 minutes to 1 hour. Refrigerate overnight.

2. Mix together all of the marinade ingredients. Rub the turkey inside and out with the marinade. Place the turkey in a very large plastic bag. We use a clean white kitchen trash bag. It's important to keep the marinade away from any metallic surface—like your turkey roasting pan. Place the (bagged) turkey in a roasting pan and marinate in the refrigerator overnight.

3. Cover the dry beans with about 4 cups water in a 2-quart saucepan. Don't add any salt yet. Bring to a boil, and boil for 5 minutes. Remove from the heat and let it stand, covered overnight.

4. The next morning, drain and rinse the beans. Add enough water to cover once again and bring to a boil; reduce heat to low, cover and cook until tender, about 35 to 50 minutes. Drain.

(continued on page 162)

(continued from page 160)

5. Rinse the rice with cold water until the water runs clear.

6. Use a large, 8-quart covered stockpot. Sauté the bacon, onion, and green pepper in the olive oil until tender.

7. Add the garlic and sauté another minute or two. Add the tomato paste, black beans, oregano, cumin, bay leaf, and vinegar. Cook for about 5 minutes, stirring gently.

8. Add the turkey stock and the rinsed rice. Bring to a boil, reduce heat to low, cover and cook for about 30 to 40 minutes, or until rice is fully cooked.

9. Finally, adjust the seasonings by adding salt and pepper to taste. Remove the bay leaf.

10. Stuff the turkey with the moros—the rice and beans you made in the previous step. Cover the turkey with bacon slices and pour wine over the top of the turkey.

11. For best results, follow the cooking instructions that come with the turkey. In general, roast the turkey at 325 degrees F until fully cooked. (Check with a meat thermometer—poultry setting). Do not overcook.

12. Remove the bacon during the last 30 minutes to allow the skin to brown.

Serves: That's a good question. The experts tell you to allow ⅓ pound of turkey per person. These "experts" have obviously never heard of the concept of leftovers. Our thinking? A 12-pound bird is going to serve no more than 10 people.

Cuban Parties: Dia de los Enamorados—Valentine's Day

Glenn: Cuba has its own version of Valentine's Day. Just like the American version, Cubans celebrate it on February 14 and the holiday has its roots in the tradition of Saint Valentine.

Jorge: However, in Cuba we call it the Día de los Enamorados, or the day of the lovers. It is a day for people involved in a love relationship . . .

Raúl: Or those who would like to get into one.

Glenn: It's like the American Valentine's Day on steroids!

Jorge: In the United States, commercial interests drive Valentine's Day: the greeting card companies, the florists, the candy companies, and so on.

Raúl: However, in Cuba, people take this day very seriously. All Cubans universally celebrate it and people really make a big deal out of it. For some people, it is the biggest holiday of the year.

Jorge: Cubans celebrate this day doing many of the things that other people do around the world—candy and flowers are popular gifts.

Glenn: And many couples enjoy a romantic dinner for two and an evening of dancing.

Raúl: One thing that sets the Cuban celebration apart is the tradition of sending "Las cartas de Amor" or letters of love.

Jorge: People consider it less than honorable to give someone a pre-printed card on the Día de los Enamorados. What most people expect is a Carta de Amor, a poetic expression of romantic love, handwritten on a card or letter.

Glenn: These expressions of love are usually very torrid and romantic.

Raúl: Not something you'd pass around for everyone to see.

Jorge: For people who have trouble writing romantic verses, there are books of verses available. You just pick the verse that is closest to your own feelings and then write it out in your own hand.

Raúl: If you want to celebrate el Día de los Enamorados, why not create a romantic Cuban dinner for two? We have several dishes in this book that you can easily cut in half to make an appropriate-size feast for you and your special someone.

Glenn: If you're young and carefree and have more than one "special someone," just prepare the full recipe.

Jorge: Just do us a favor and don't brag about it!

Pollo al Ajillo de Jorge
Jorge's Chicken in Garlic Sauce

Glenn: Just about every Cuban restaurant in Miami makes a version of this dish.

Jorge: Very few Cuban dishes don't include a healthy dose of garlic. It adds such a great flavor to everything.

Glenn: When my sister Diane was first dating her future husband Dick, he invited her over for some chili that he had prepared from a new recipe. The only problem—he wasn't sure what a "clove" of garlic was. He ended up adding three HEADS of garlic to the dish, instead of three cloves!

Raúl: I don't know but that actually sounds like it would be tasty!

Jorge: As with all white meat chicken, you want to be very careful not to overcook this.

Glenn: So try to limit the conversation and maximize the chicken watching.

¼ cup olive oil
2 pounds whole boneless, skinless chicken breast, cut into ¼-inch-thick slices
1 teaspoon salt
¼ teaspoon pepper
White flour for dredging
8 cloves garlic, minced
¼ cup chicken broth
¼ cup white wine
1 tablespoon lemon juice
4 tablespoons butter
2 tablespoons cornstarch mixed with ¼ cup water to thicken
¼ cup chopped cilantro

1. Preheat the oven to 250 degrees F. ("Keep warm" temperature.)

2. Heat the olive oil in a large sauté pan.

3. Season the chicken pieces with salt and pepper. Dredge the chicken in the flour and place the flour-coated pieces in the pan; begin browning on one side over medium-high heat.

4. Cook on one side for approximately 2 minutes, flip all of the pieces over, and add the garlic. Continue to sauté until the chicken is cooked through. Do not overcook.

5. Remove the chicken, place in a covered pan and put in the oven to keep warm.

6. De-glaze the pan by adding the chicken broth, wine, and lemon juice. Reduce heat to medium-low and whisk constantly to make a smooth sauce. Add the butter and cook just long enough to blend. The sauce should be slightly thick. If the sauce is a bit thin, tighten it up with a little cornstarch dissolved in water.

7. Place the cooked chicken back in the sauce. Sprinkle with the chopped cilantro and serve hot.

Serves 4

Pollo de la Plancha
Grilled Chicken Breasts

Glenn: Pollo de la Plancha is a long-time Cuban favorite that pre-dates America's flight from red meat during the famous "Red Scare" of the 1990s.

Raúl: Those were frightening times, with evil pieces of red meat—the red menace—lurking on every corner.

Jorge: We never bought into the "red meat is bad" movement. We love our steaks too much to go along with that.

Glenn: In any case, the Red Scare made an instant hero out of the boneless, skinless chicken breast. It started turning up on restaurant menus all over the United States.

Raúl: Cubans were way ahead of the wave; we have enjoyed the grilled chicken breast for ages.

Jorge: And it has nothing to do with health reasons, they just taste good.

4 whole boneless chicken breasts
Fresh lime juice
Salt and pepper
Cumin
Flour for dredging

½ cup finely chopped white onion
¼ cup olive oil
4 cloves garlic, finely chopped
¼ cup chopped fresh cilantro

1. Sprinkle a little water on the chicken breasts and place (one at a time) on a piece of plastic wrap. Fold the plastic wrap over to make a little pouch.

2. Place the pouch on a cutting board and beat with a smooth meat mallet or rolling pin until very thin. Don't go crazy with the hammer. You want a thin chicken breast, not ground chicken. If your chicken breasts are very thick, you'll want to slice them in half lengthwise before pounding them out.

3. Remove the plastic wrap and dry the chicken with a paper towel. Sprinkle it with a little lime juice. Shake on some salt, pepper, and cumin by eye.

4. Dredge the chicken breasts in the flour, shaking off any excess. You want a very thin layer of flour.

5. Sauté the onion briefly in a large sauté pan over medium heat—just long enough to heat through and coat with a little oil. Add a pinch of salt and a little pepper to the onions as they cook. Add the garlic during the last minute or two of sautéing. Use a slotted spoon to remove the onion and garlic and set aside.

6. Increase the heat to high. Toss in the chicken breasts and fry the chicken, browning on both sides.

7. The chicken should cook very quickly—do not overcook. Just a few minutes on each side should do it. Just make a small slice in one of the breasts to make sure it's cooked through.

8. To serve, cover each breast with the cooked onions and garlic. Add a squeeze of fresh lime juice and some fresh cilantro. Serve over rice.

Serves 4

166

Pollo al Chilindrón
Chicken with Tomatoes and Peppers

Jorge: This dish comes from the Aragon region of Spain.

Glenn: We've enjoyed a very similar dish in Cuban-Chinese restaurants, except it had more of an Asian flavor.

Jorge: The Chino-Latino version used ginger and soy sauce, while this Cuban dish gets its flavor from paprika, cumin, and of course a sofrito.

Raúl: This recipe produces delicious tender chicken in a thick, hearty sauce. I love it.

Glenn: Make sure to cut your peppers and onions in large chunks. This isn't the time to try to hide the onions and peppers from anyone in your party who may fear them.

4 strips smoked bacon, chopped
Salt and pepper to taste
8 boneless skinless chicken thighs, cut in thirds
Flour for dusting
¼ cup olive oil
1 cup chopped green bell pepper
1 cup chopped yellow onion
4 cloves garlic, minced
½ cup white wine

1 (16-ounce) can whole tomatoes, quartered, with juice
1 tablespoon sweet Spanish paprika
1 tablespoon cumin
1 teaspoon salt
½ teaspoon black pepper
2 tablespoons cornstarch dissolved in ½ cup water to thicken
½ cup green peas

1. Sauté the bacon long enough to brown and render the fat. Remove the bacon.

2. Salt and pepper the chicken thighs on both sides, dredge in flour, and shake off any excess. Brown in the bacon fat, remove chicken, and set aside.

3. Add the olive oil to the pan and sauté the green pepper and onion until limp. Add garlic during the last minute or two only.

4. Place the vegetable mixture in a large covered pot and add the wine, tomatoes, and tomato juice.

5. Stir in the paprika, cumin, salt, and pepper; return the chicken thighs and bacon to the pan.

6. Bring to a boil, reduce heat to low, and simmer, uncovered, until chicken is fully cooked and tender, about 25 to 35 minutes. Remove chicken and keep hot.

7. Tighten up the sauce with a little cornstarch mixed with water. You want a thick, rich sauce. Finally toss in the green peas and immediately remove sauce from heat.

8. Serve chicken pieces over white rice with plenty of sauce on top.

Serves 4

Of Caldo Concentrado and Vino Seco

No Cuban kitchen would be complete without a supply of caldo concentrado (bouillon cubes) and vino seco, a dry red cooking wine. The only problem with these two ingredients is that they are loaded with sodium. Although bouillon cubes turned up regularly in Cuban dishes, many Cuban abuelas, or grandmothers, made their own stocks with real meat. You can simmer beef bones and trimmings, chicken bones

and skin, a hambone and so on in water to create a delicious and natural stock.

Although Cuban abuelas occasionally went natural with the meat stocks, when it came to vino seco they accepted no substitutes. Check out the pantry of any well stocked Cuban kitchen in Miami and you'll find a bottle or too of these "Spanish style" cooking wines. When most Cuban cooks talk about cooking

sherry, they're really talking about vino seco.

We normally recommend using a good red or white wine in your Cuban dishes. However, if you grew up in a Cuban household and you really want to make it just like your mom or grandmother did, go ahead and reach for the vino seco. And that goes for the bouillon cubes as well! You may want to adjust the salt . . .

Asado al la Parrilla de Patio

Backyard Grilling

Costillitas
Cuban Style Baby Back Ribs

Glenn: Your local chain restaurant does not have a lock on the baby back rib franchise.

Glenn: Your local chain restaurant does not have a lock on the baby back rib franchise.

Jorge: Quite the contrary, you can make your own great baby back ribs in the privacy of your own home.

Raúl: With no corporate intervention.

Jorge: And with nobody singing an annoying song!

Glenn: In this recipe, you pre-cook the ribs on the stovetop and then finish them on the grill.

Jorge: The trip to the grill gives these beauties those attractive grill marks and that great grilled taste.

2 or 3 whole racks baby back ribs
2½ cups brown sugar, divided
2 lemons, quartered
2 limes, quartered
2 tablespoons allspice

5 cloves garlic, mashed
1 whole onion sliced
2 teaspoons salt
2 cups water
Water to cover the meat

GUAVA SAUCE

½ cup guava jelly
½ cup brown sugar
Juice of 1 lime

1 teaspoon vinegar
1 teaspoon ground cumin
½ teaspoon salt

1. Trim the white membrane off the backside of the ribs and cut them into smaller-size sections— either in half or in thirds.

2. Get a large 8-quart saucepan and add 2 cups brown sugar, lemons, limes, allspice, garlic, onion, and salt. As you add the lemons and limes, squeeze as much juice as you can into the pot and drop them in, peel and all. Add water and stir until some of the sugar has dissolved.

3. Add the rib sections to the pan. Add enough additional water to cover. Bring to a boil; reduce heat to low and simmer, covered, for 1 hour.

MEANWHILE . . .

1. Make the sauce by placing all of the sauce ingredients in a 3-quart saucepan.

2. Bring to a boil, stirring constantly for 5 minutes.

3. Reduce heat to low and simmer, uncovered, for 15 minutes. Let cool.

4. Assuming your ribs are ready, now it's time to fire up the grill. When the grill is good and hot, lightly oil the grill surface to avoid any sticking.

5. Place the ribs meaty side down on the grill and let cook for about 5 minutes, making sure that they do not burn. Adjust your heat source accordingly.

6. Turn the ribs over so that the meaty side is up. Sprinkle the meat with some salt, pepper, and some of the remaining brown sugar. Continue to cook the ribs on the grill for another 5 to 10 minutes.

7. The ribs are completely cooked when you remove them from the stovetop. We just want to brown them and give them a nice grilled flavor. Remember that sugar burns easily and burnt sugar tastes terrible, so keep an eye out for any flare-ups.

(continued on page 174)

(continued from page 172)

8. We frequently double and triple this recipe to serve a large party. However, you probably need two grills or a lot of patient party-goers if you want to keep everyone happy.

9. Serve the ribs hot off the grill, with the Guava Sauce on the side.

Serves 4

CUBAN CHARCOAL

Jorge: In Cuba, you had to make your own charcoal, a long and laborious process that involves starting logs on fire and partially burying them or placing them in a box called a carbonero *so they smolder and burn incompletely. When Raúl first came to the United States, he thought that this was the way people did it all over the world.*

Glenn: Imagine his surprise when Jorge took him to a local supermarket and showed him bags and bags of charcoal all neatly packaged and stacked from floor to ceiling.

Raúl: Wow, man I couldn't believe it!

Jorge: The homemade charcoal does give the pig a distinctive taste.

Glenn: But only a real diehard or the Cuban Martha Stewart would even think of attempting this feat today.

Lechón Asado
Roast Pork

1 "fresh ham," bone in and skin on, or have your butcher butterfly it or use 1 pork shoulder roast

Mojo (see page 191)
Salt and black pepper

1. Pierce the roast as many times as you can with a sharp knife or fork. Use a sharp knife to cut several slits, or pockets, in the meat, but DO NOT cut through any skin.

2. Pour Mojo (save a little for roasting) over the pork. Stuff the crushed garlic from the mojo into all of the slits you made in the meat. Cover, and let sit in refrigerator overnight.

3. The next day, remove the roast from the marinade and lightly salt and pepper.

4. Use a covered grill, such as the Weber kettle or a covered gas grill. Bank the coals to each side, leaving an empty space beneath your ham. On a gas grill, use front or rear burners only to cook with indirect heat.

5. Place the roast fat side up on the grill. Spoon extra marinade over the roast occasionally as it cooks. If not using a gas grill, add charcoal to the sides as needed to maintain roasting temperature.

6. Remove the roast from the grill when the temperature reaches 155 degrees F.

7. Immediately cover with foil and let rest for 10 minutes before slicing and serving. The roast will continue to cook after you remove it from the heat.

Serves: Allow about ¼ to ½ pound per person, depending on side dishes

Jorge: If you are having a big party, there is no substitute for roasting a whole pig.

Raúl: We just couldn't do a Cuban party book without including our recipe for roast pork.

Jorge: You find pork like this at just about every Cuban party.

Glenn: Yes, we really recommend that you do your party right by roasting a whole pig as we describe on our website: Cuban-Christmas.com.

Jorge: However, we do understand that there may be times when you just can't do a whole pig.

Glenn: In these cases, you can make Lechón Asado on the grill using this recipe.

Puerco Asado Estilo Chino-Cubano
Chinese-Cuban Style Pork Roast

Glenn: We regularly hear from our Chinese-Cuban friends who enjoy our website and are grateful that we have not forgotten the Chinese influence on Cuban cuisine.

Raúl: This recipe is an adaptation of a couple of similar recipes that readers have sent to us over the years.

Jorge: Most recipes call for this to be made in the oven, but we have found that it is a great dish to prepare outside on the grill.

Glenn: Years ago when we first started making this recipe, it was hard to find hoisin sauce and five-spice powder.

Jorge: Now, just about every supermarket in America carries these Asian products!

GLAZE

¼ cup orange juice
¼ cup lemon juice
1 cup honey

ROAST

1 5-pound pork roast (a pernil, fresh ham, or our favorite for this dish, a pork shoulder, all work well here)
½ cup cooked black beans
2 tablespoons orange juice
2 tablespoons soy sauce
2 tablespoons sherry
¼ cup sugar
2 tablespoons hoisin sauce
2 tablespoons five-spice powder
5 cloves garlic, minced

FOR THE GLAZE

1. Make your glaze by adding all of the glaze ingredients to a 3-quart saucepan. Bring to a rolling boil and let boil for about 5 minutes, stirring constantly. Reduce heat to low and simmer, uncovered, for about 15 minutes.

FOR THE ROAST

1. We like to use a pork shoulder, or what is sometimes called a "Boston Butt" roast. The pork shoulder does have a large bone, but the meat is very tender. You may also use a pernil, which is the back leg of the pig. You also may use a "fresh" ham, which is the same as a pernil except that the lower leg bone and surrounding meat have been removed.

2. Wash your pork roast thoroughly and pat dry with a paper towel.

3. Mash up the cooked black beans in a mixing bowl. Then add orange juice, soy sauce, sherry, sugar, hoisin sauce, five-spice powder, and garlic. Mix everything together. Spoon this mixture to cover the outside of the roast.

4. Preheat your outdoor charcoal or gas grill. You'll want to use the indirect heat method to cook this roast. On a covered charcoal grill, bank your coals to the sides of the grill, leaving a section with no charcoal beneath it. On a three- or four-burner gas grill, light only the side burners or front and back burners. On a two-burner gas grill, just light one burner.

5. Place the pork roast on the unheated side of the grill and close the cover. On a gas grill, adjust the flame so that the grill temperature is approximately 300 degrees F.

(continued on page 179)

(continued from page 176)

6. After the first 20 minutes of roasting, baste your pork roast every 15 minutes with the glaze mixture. After about an hour on the grill, test for doneness with a meat thermometer. Remove the roast from the grill when the temperature reaches 155 degrees F.

7. Remove the roast to a serving platter and lightly tent the roast with some aluminum foil sprayed with cooking spray. This will allow the meat to continue cooking for about 10 to 15 minutes. The spray and the light touch with the tenting will help keep the aluminum foil from sticking to the glaze.

8. Carve with a sharp knife and serve hot with your favorite side dishes.

Serves 6 to 8

THE VOLCANO: THE ORIGINAL BACKYARD COOKER

The volcano was a common sight in backyards in Cuba, and today many Cuban Americans carry on the tradition. It's an outdoor single-burner stove, with the burner sized to fit a large cooking pot. You can fill the pot with oil for deep-frying or water for boiling. Many people prefer to fry fish outdoors—it keeps the smell out of the house, and some people think the abundance of fresh air outside actually makes the fish taste better. For par-

ties, you can use a volcano and a large pot of water to boil up a huge batch of yuca.

Volcanoes in Cuba were usually fueled with wood or charcoal, although some people made volcanoes that used kerosene. Lighting the kerosene-fueled volcano is not an easy task. A pump pressurized the kerosene. It looked a little like a bicycle pump and the user had to pump this handle several times before lighting the stove. You added a small

quantity of alcohol to a tray in the center of the gas ring.

You lit the alcohol on fire, waited awhile to make sure the flame was steady and then you opened a little valve to release the kerosene gas. If you were lucky, the kerosene gas would pop to life with a steady blue flame. If not, the gas would fizzle and smoke and you had to go through the entire procedure all over again.

Pescado Asado Three Guys
Grilled Fish Three Guys Style

Glenn: We came up with a Peruvian-inspired recipe that uses a marinade to infuse the fish with delicious spices.

Raúl: This recipe works great with just about any type of fish fillet. Make sure to leave the skin on the fish.

Jorge: The skin will keep the fillets from shrinking and will keep the fish from sticking to the grill.

Glenn: Once you have cooked the fish, you can easily remove the skin before serving. Or leave it on if you like it that way.

MARINADE

½ cup olive oil
Juice of one lime
Juice of one lemon
6 cloves garlic, crushed
¼ cup chopped cilantro
1 teaspoon oregano

1 bunch green onions, chopped
1 teaspoon salt
½ teaspoon ground black pepper
1 teaspoon red pepper flakes
Salt and pepper to taste

Fish fillets: salmon, snapper, swordfish, yellowtail—anything you like with the skin on. We love to make this with a large 2- to 3-pound salmon fillet. If you use smaller fish, consider grilling an individual fillet for each of your guests.

1. Put everything (except the fish!) in a non-metallic bowl and mix with a spoon to make the marinade.

2. Place fish in a shallow non-metallic pan and cover with the marinade. Cover pan with plastic wrap and refrigerate for no more than 2 hours. Remove fish from marinade.

3. Make sure your grill surface is clean and well oiled. Set up your gas or charcoal grill so that you have a section of grill surface with no source of direct heat beneath it. (Bank the coals to the side of a charcoal grill, or turn off the middle or end burners on a gas grill.)

4. Drizzle a little olive oil on the fillet and place it on the hot side of the grill skin side up just long enough to put some nice grill marks on the flesh.

5. Then carefully use a steel spatula to flip the fillet skin-side down on the cooler section of the grill. Try to cook the fish at a low heat — "low and slow" is definitely the way to go!

6. Cover your grill and continue cooking until the fish flakes with a fork. Keep an eye on the fish so it doesn't burn. Salt and pepper to taste.

Serves: Allow approximately ½ to ¾ pound per person depending on your side dishes. The marinade recipe makes enough for approximately three pounds of fish fillets.

Pinchos

Jorge: **We love to grill out!** It's a great way to enjoy the outdoors and enjoy some great food at the same time.

Raúl: **And it sure beats jogging!**

Glenn: **The great thing is,** once you get them on the grill, pinchos cook fast. This leaves you with plenty of time for enjoying the beverage of your choice and some good conversation as you dig into your delicious pinchos with everyone else.

Raúl: **Instead of "slaving"** over the grill while everyone else enjoys the shade!

Jorge: **You can put everything together for some delicious pinchos in less than an hour's prep time.**

Raúl: **And that includes** drinking a beer or two.

Pinchos de Camarones—Shrimp Kabobs

5 cloves garlic, mashed with ½ teaspoon salt and ½ teaspoon black peppercorns
¼ cup olive oil
1 tablespoon lime juice
½ teaspoon ground cumin
2 pounds shrimp, peeled, deveined, and butterflied

1. Mash garlic, salt, and peppercorns into a paste using a mortar and pestle.
2. Combine all ingredients except the shrimp in a non-metallic bowl.
3. Add the butterflied shrimp and toss gently to coat.
4. Marinate in the refrigerator for about 3 to 4 hours.
5. Cook as described on page 186.

Serves 4

Pinchos de Carne—Beef Kabobs

10 cloves garlic, mashed with 2 teaspoons salt and 1 teaspoon black peppercorns
1 cup orange juice
½ cup lemon juice
½ cup lime juice
½ cup minced onion
1 teaspoon ground oregano
1 cup Spanish olive oil
4 pounds top sirloin, cubed for kabobs

1. Mash garlic, salt, and peppercorns into a paste using a mortar and pestle.
2. Stir in the juices, onion, and oregano.
3. Let sit at room temperature for 30 minutes.
4. Heat the olive oil in a 2-quart saucepan until hot, but not deep-frying hot. We're looking for something in the neighborhood of 300 degrees F. If it starts to smoke, it's too hot! Remove the oil from heat and quickly (and carefully) whisk in the garlic-orange juice mixture until well blended. Let cool.
5. Place the sirloin cubes in a non-metallic bowl. Pour the marinade over the meat, cover the bowl with plastic wrap, and refrigerate at least 4 hours, but preferably overnight.
6. Cook as described on page 186.

Serves 6 to 8

PINCHOS DE POLLO—CHICKEN KABOBS

2 tablespoons grated lemon peel

¼ cup lemon juice

½ cup olive oil

5 cloves garlic, minced

¼ cup lime juice

1 teaspoon salt

½ teaspoon red pepper flakes

½ cup real mayonnaise

3 pounds chicken (see step 2 below)

1. Whisk together all ingredients except chicken in a non-metallic bowl.

2. For chicken, you can use light or dark meat or do what we do and make both. Buy boneless, skinless chicken thighs for your dark meat and boneless, skinless chicken breasts for the white.

3. The key is not mixing the dark and white meat on the same skewer. Chicken breast meat needs to be cooked perfectly on the grill with little margin for error—so keep an eye on your white meat. If you overcook it, it's going to be dry. Dark meat is a little more forgiving.

4. Skewer the meat directly from the marinade. Do not rinse, pat dry, or otherwise cause the thick marinade to part company with the chicken pieces.

5. Cook as described on page 186.

Serves 6 to 8

PINCHOS DE PUERCO—PORK KABOBS

1 cup finely diced onion

6 cloves garlic, mashed with 2 teaspoons salt and 1 teaspoon black peppercorns

3 tablespoons sweet Spanish paprika

2 teaspoons ground cumin

1 cup olive oil

½ cup lemon juice

¼ cup white wine

4 pounds boneless pork, cubed for kabobs

1. Make your marinade by combining all the ingredients except pork in a non-metallic bowl.

2. Add the pork cubes and mix them around until well coated with the marinade.

3. Cover the bowl with plastic wrap and refrigerate overnight.

4. Skewer the meat loosely so there is a little breathing room between the pork pieces.

5. Cook as described on page 186.

Serves 8

To Cook the Pinchos

1. Assembling and cooking the pinchos is basically the same, no matter what meat or seafood you use. If you are using wooden skewers, soak them in water before using.

2. Skewer the meat or seafood onto the skewers.

3. Get your grill nice and hot.

4. Grill the meat or shrimp, turning occasionally, according to cooking times below, or until cooked to perfection. If you enjoy a more spicy hot flavor, be sure to brush the pinchos occasionally with Raúl and Glenn's Pincho Oil (see next page).

5. Adjust seasonings as you go—meaning a little salt and black pepper is usually in order.

NOTE: We know that many people like to make their pinchos with chunks of onion, green or red bell pepper, and cherry tomatoes, or even zucchini. This tradition got started in restaurants where they wanted to make a pleasing presentation and disguise the fact that you weren't getting very much meat with your order. The problem with this method is that the vegetables tend to cook a lot faster than the meats. If you want to grill some vegetables with your pinchos, make up some separate skewers with veggies only. A good rule of thumb is to toss the vegetable pinchos on the grill about midway through the meat cooking times listed below.

TIP: For those who are "resistant to work or exertion"—otherwise known as lazy—skip the skewers. When we make pinchos for a large group, we frequently toss out the skewers and just put the meat chunks or shrimp directly on the grill. We can then serve the pinchos "family-style" in serving bowls garnished with our grilled onions, green and red bell peppers, and cherry tomatoes. Just make sure your chunks are big enough to prevent them from slipping through the grill.

Cooking times:

Cook pork until cooked through and juices run clear, about 8 to 12 minutes.

Cook chicken until cooked through and juices run clear, approximately 6 to 12 minutes, being especially careful not to overcook any white meat.

Cook beef exactly as you like it from very rare to well done—anywhere from 2 to 12 minutes.

Cook shrimp until they turn pink or translucent, approximately 2 to 4 minutes.

Raúl and Glenn's Pincho Oil

5 cloves garlic, minced
¾ cup olive oil
2 teaspoons ground cumin
1 teaspoon sweet or smoked paprika
1 teaspoon ground oregano

¼ cup lemon juice
¼ cup lime juice
2 teaspoons hot sauce (Tabasco style)
Rum (optional)
Salt and pepper to taste

1. Whisk all of the ingredients together in a non-metallic bowl.

2. Season to taste with salt and pepper.

3. Rum is an optional ingredient. If Raúl and Glenn happen to be drinking rum and grilling at the same time, some of the rum usually finds its way into the pincho oil.

4. Use this oil to baste the meat or seafood occasionally as it cooks on the grill. It also tastes great on those vegetable kabobs.

NOTE: Pincho oil is quite volatile, so apply it sparingly to your meat or seafood and watch for flare-ups.

Pollo a la Parilla
Grilled Chicken

Glenn: When we just don't have time to roast a whole pig, we like to grill chicken in the same style.

Raúl: We also make a few chickens when we are roasting a pig for our friends who don't eat pork.

Jorge: We prepare the chicken the same way we would make a whole pig or lechón, marinated overnight in the refrigerator with plenty of mojo.

Glenn: A dash or two of cumin helps bring out that great Latin roasted chicken flavor.

2 whole frying chickens
Mojo (see page 191)
Salt

Black pepper
Cumin

1. Use a meat cleaver to split the chickens in half.

2. Remove the "giblets"—the heart, liver, gizzard, spleen, and any other internal organs that may have found their way into your bird and wash the chicken thoroughly under cold running water.

3. Place the chicken halves in a non-metallic bowl, cover with Mojo, and refrigerate overnight. Reserve a little bit of the marinade to use on the chicken while grilling.

4. Remove the chicken from the marinade and pat dry with a paper towel. Discard marinade.

5. Lightly salt and pepper the chicken halves and dust on a little cumin.

6. If you happen to be roasting a whole pig, just place the chicken halves on the pigholder—wherever you can find room. The slow fire of the pig roaster means that your chicken will come out perfectly roasted and juicy at the same time as the pig. You can use a meat thermometer to make sure.

7. If you're not roasting a pig (and we have only one question for you—why not?), use a covered grill, such as the Weber kettle or a covered gas grill. Bank the coals to each side, leaving an empty space beneath your chickens. On a gas grill, use front or rear burners only. The idea is to cook with indirect heat.

8. Spoon extra marinade over the chickens occasionally as they roast. If not using a gas grill, add charcoal to the sides as needed to maintain roasting temperature. Use a meat thermometer to determine when the chicken is fully cooked—the temperature should reach 175 degrees F and the chicken juices will run clear.

Serves 4 to 6

Mojo
Cuban Marinade

8 to 10 cloves garlic
1 teaspoon salt
½ teaspoon whole black peppercorns

1 teaspoon oregano
¾ cup sour orange juice

1. The key to making mojo is in the proportions. Keep all the ingredients in approximately the proportions of the basic recipe above and you can't go wrong. The nice thing is you can make exactly the amount you need.

2. Use a mortar and pestle. Add a few cloves of garlic, a little salt, some black peppercorns, and some oregano. Mash them all together into a paste. Scoop the paste out into a separate bowl. Continue this process until all of the garlic is mashed.

3. Stir in ¾ cup sour orange juice. Let sit at room temperature for 30 minutes or longer. Use immediately to season your meat, or refrigerate for later use.

   TIP: If you are making your own "sour" orange juice and it doesn't taste very tart, add a little white vinegar.

Serves: Make any amount from enough marinade for a small fresh ham to a whole hog large enough to frighten small children!

Jorge: The secret ingredient in Cuban cooking? It's mojo, a unique marinade that gives many dishes a distinctive garlic and citrus flavor.

Glenn: It should therefore come as no surprise that you make a mojo marinade from garlic and citrus.

Jorge: Thank you Sherlock Holmes for your brilliant deduction.

Raúl: Mojo is another recipe that uses the sour orange, an almost bitter orange that grows throughout Cuba.

Glenn: Sour orange can be hard to find outside of South Florida. Some Latin groceries sell naranja agria (bitter orange) juice in bottles.

Jorge: Or use our standard sour orange substitute of regular orange, lemon, and lime juice (see page 144).

Acompañamientos

Side Dishes

Arroz Amarillo
Yellow Rice

8 saffron strands
¼ cup hot water
¼ cup olive oil
1 cup finely chopped onion
3 cups parboiled rice

1 teaspoon salt
½ teaspoon cumin
1 teaspoon dried oregano
4½ cups chicken broth
3 tablespoons butter, at room temperature

1. Crush the saffron strands and let them steep for about 20 minutes in hot water to make saffron "tea." Run the tea through a strainer. Keep the saffron water and toss out anything that remains in the strainer.

2. Heat the olive oil in a large saucepan and sauté the onion until translucent. Stir in the rice and salt and sauté briefly, until the rice begins to brown slightly.

3. Add the cumin, oregano, chicken broth, and saffron water, and bring to a boil. Lower heat and cook, uncovered, until the rice has absorbed some of the broth.

4. Cover and cook over low heat for about 20 to 30 minutes, or until the rice is soft and fluffy. Just before serving, stir in 3 tablespoons butter and fluff with a fork.

5. You can press the rice into a salad mold or use an ice cream scoop to create a nice presentation.

Serves 8

Jorge: Just about every Cuban meal includes frijoles negros and rice.

Glenn: However, we know that some people just can't, or won't eat beans. The "bean-a-phobic" people at your dinner party are limited to eating plain white rice . . .

Raúl: . . . and nothing is more boring than plain white rice.

Jorge: Our solution? Make up a batch of Arroz Amarillo as a tasty side dish.

Glenn: We must warn you, however, never serve black beans with yellow rice. They do this in Tampa all the time, but in Miami, it is a major blunder.

Raúl: It's like serving filet mignon with ketchup on it.

Arroz con Garbanzos
Rice with Garbanzo Beans

Jorge: For a delicious change of pace, we really love to eat rice with garbanzo beans.

Glenn: Maybe you're just getting a little tired of eating all of those black beans every day.

Raúl: No Cuban ever gets tired of black beans!

Jorge: Yes, we can easily eat black beans for breakfast, lunch, and dinner.

Glenn: In any case, Arroz con Garbanzos is a nice, traditional dish without a single black bean.

1 pound garbanzo beans, cleaned and rinsed
2 cups diced onions
1 cup diced red bell pepper
1 cup diced green bell pepper
¼ cup olive oil
6 cloves garlic, mashed
1 Spanish chorizo link, sliced
2 cups parboiled rice

½ teaspoon Bijol powder
3 cups chicken broth
½ cup white wine
½ cup tomato puree
1 teaspoon sweet Spanish paprika
1 teaspoon salt
¼ teaspoon black pepper
1 cup diced Roma tomatoes

1. Put the beans in a large pot, cover with cold water, and let soak overnight.

2. Drain the beans, cover them with fresh water, and toss in a shot of olive oil—about a tablespoon.

3. Bring the beans to a boil over high heat, then reduce heat to medium-low, and simmer for 40 to 60 minutes, or until the beans are cooked and soft.

4. Make a sofrito by sautéing onion and red and green peppers in olive oil over low heat until the onions are translucent.

5. Add the garlic and chorizo and cook just a minute or two more, stirring occasionally.

6. Place the sofrito, chorizo, garbanzo beans, rice, Bijol powder, chicken broth, wine, tomato puree, paprika, salt, and pepper in a large saucepan or stockpot. (Save the diced tomatoes for the end.)

7. Bring to a boil over high heat and cook, uncovered, for 2 to 3 minutes. Immediately cover, reduce heat to low, and simmer for about 20 to 30 minutes, or until the rice is fully cooked.

8. Fluff the cooked rice with a fork, fold in the diced fresh tomato, and serve hot.

Serves 6 to 8

Cóctel de Frutas Tropical
Tropical Fruit Cocktail

Glenn: For many Americans, fruit cocktail is that over-cooked fruit that comes in a can.

Jorge: Yes, even in Cuba we had canned fruit cocktail.

Glenn: We're sure that canned fruit cocktail has a place in this world; we've just never been able to figure out exactly what it's good for.

Raúl: Who needs canned fruit when we have plenty of fresh fruit as close as our backyard?

Glenn: This recipe features fresh, ripe tropical fruits and a little Three Guys From Miami twist.

Jorge: You're guests will really be amazed.

1 cup orange juice
1 cup apple juice
1 tablespoon lemon juice
½ cup brown sugar
½ teaspoon grated lemon peel
2 cinnamon sticks
1 tablespoon cornstarch mixed with water

2 sweet oranges, peeled and sectioned
2 cups cubed ripe fruta bomba (papaya)
2 cups cubed ripe mango
2 cups fresh pineapple chunks
½ cup sweetened coconut flakes
Mint leaves for garnish

1. In a 3-quart saucepan, combine juices, sugar, and grated lemon peel. Add cinnamon sticks.

2. Bring to a rolling boil, and let boil for 5 minutes, stirring constantly. Reduce heat to low, whisk in the cornstarch/water mixture, and simmer, uncovered, for 10 to 15 minutes. The sauce should reduce and thicken.

3. Remove cinnamon sticks and let the sauce cool to room temperature.

4. Meanwhile, cut up your delicious tropical fruit. Make sure that the fruit is very ripe and naturally sweet.

5. Toss all the fruit and the coconut together in a large bowl. Add the room-temperature sauce and toss gently.

6. Cover and place in the refrigerator until completely chilled.

7. Take your salad out of the refrigerator and garnish with mint leaves.

Serves 8

Congri
Cuban Red Beans and Rice

1 pound dried small red beans
1 ham bone (shank end) with plenty of
    meat or 3 cups ham chunks
5 cups water
1 cup red wine
4 strips bacon, chopped
Olive oil for frying
2 cups diced yellow onion
2 cups diced green bell pepper
5 cloves garlic, minced

1 teaspoon cumin
1 teaspoon oregano
1 bay leaf
3 tablespoons vinegar
1 habanero pepper, quartered or 2 jalapeño
    peppers, sliced lengthwise
2 teaspoons salt
¼ teaspoon black pepper
3 cups parboiled white rice

Jorge: Although similar to moros y cristianos, you make the traditional Congri of Cuba Oriente (the Eastern provinces of Cuba) with red beans.

Glenn: Not only do the Oriente Cubans use red beans instead of black, they give it an extra kick with a habanero pepper or two.

Raúl: It is a very good dish. Congri is a nice change of pace from all of the black beans that we eat at home.

1. Cover the dried beans with water in a large pot. Bring to a boil, then remove beans from heat, cover, and let them soak overnight.

2. The next day, drain the beans and cover them with fresh water. Bring to a boil, reduce heat to low, cover, and cook until tender, about 1 hour. Drain.

3. While your beans are cooking, place your ham bone in a separate large pot with the water and wine and a pinch of salt. You may substitute 2 or 3 cups of ham if you don't have a ham bone. Bring to a boil, reduce heat to low, cover, and simmer for about 1 hour. If using ham chunks, reduce this cooking time to 20 to 30 minutes.

4. Remove the ham bone or ham chunks and keep the liquid. Remove all of the meat from the bone and break into small chunks.

5. Use a large, covered cooking pot. Begin by frying the bacon pieces in a little olive oil until they begin to crisp. Add the onion and green pepper and a little more oil and sauté until the onions are tender. Add the garlic and ham chunks and cook another minute or two.

6. Add the beans, cumin, oregano, bay leaf, vinegar, habanero or jalapeños, salt, pepper, and 4 cups (measure exactly) of the stock you made when you cooked the ham. (If you're short on stock, add a little water to make up the difference.)

7. Rinse the rice with cold water until the water runs clear. Add the rinsed rice and bring to a boil.

8. Reduce heat to low, cover, and cook over low heat—stirring once or twice in the first 5 minutes only—about 30 to 45 minutes, until the rice is fully cooked.

9. Remove the habanero or jalapeño pepper and the bay leaf. Adjust the seasonings to taste.

TIP: We frequently "forget" to remove the hot peppers from the plate of an annoying (and unsuspecting) in-law!

Serves 6 to 8

Ensalada de Aguacate
Avocado Salad

Glenn: We usually use the Florida avocado in our salads. It's the large light green avocado that looks a little like a big, fat mango.

Jorge: If you can find a Florida avocado in your area, great. You can even impress the local food police in your neighborhood by telling them that the Florida avocado has less fat than dark-skinned avocados.

Glenn: I have never lost a minute of sleep worrying about the fat in an avocado!

Raúl: The Florida avocado also has a lighter, crisper flavor than the Hass avocado.

Glenn: Make sure your avocado is ripe before you peel it. A toothpick should easily pierce the soft flesh.

1 cup diced green or red bell pepper
3 cups ripe Florida avocado, sliced
   (substitute Hass avocados if you must)

½ cup sliced sweet red or yellow onion
Salt and pepper to taste
Fresh cilantro, chopped

Dressing
¼ cup olive oil
¼ cup fresh lime juice

½ teaspoon cumin
Pepper to taste

1. Blanch the green pepper by putting it in a small bowl and microwaving on high for approximately 45 seconds. Let cool.

2. Make the dressing by whisking together the olive oil and lemon juice with the cumin and a little fresh ground pepper.

3. Gently toss the avocado with the green pepper, onion, and dressing. Add salt and pepper to taste.

   TIP: "Gently Toss the Avocado" is a great game to play in the backyard with the kids.

4. Artfully arrange the salad ingredients on a chilled plate. Sprinkle with cilantro.

Serves 6

Ensalada de Arroz Frío
Cold Rice Salad

Glenn: Potato salad may be the most popular salad for American backyard barbecues and picnics, but Cubans have a nice alternative.

Raúl: We make a delicious salad with our own favorite starch—rice of course.

Jorge: This recipe is great because you make it the day before when you are still feeling ambitious and serve it the next day when all you want to do is take it easy.

4 cups cooked rice
2 cups chopped green onion
2 cups chopped green bell pepper
2 cups chopped green olives

1 cup green peas, raw
2 cups chopped sweet pickle
2 cups chopped dill pickle
6 hard-boiled eggs, chopped

DRESSING
⅓ cup olive oil
⅓ cup lime juice
1½ teaspoons ground cumin

2 cups real mayonnaise
2 hard-boiled eggs, whole
Salt and pepper to taste

1. Toss the cooked rice with the onion, green pepper, olives, peas, and pickles.

2. Make the dressing by placing the olive oil, lime juice, and cumin in a blender and whipping until the oil and juice are emulsified.

3. Add the mayonnaise and 2 hard-boiled eggs (shells removed, of course) and continue to process until well blended.

4. Salt and pepper the dressing to taste.

5. Mix the dressing with the rice mixture. Gently fold in the 6 hard-boiled eggs.

6. Refrigerate for a minimum of 4 hours, but preferably overnight.

7. Serve chilled and keep cold. The salad that is!

Serves 8

Ensalada Cubana con Camarones
Cuban Salad with Shrimp

6 strips bacon, chopped
Salt and pepper
1 pound small shrimp, peeled and deveined
1 teaspoon ground cumin

2 ripe red tomatoes
1 red onion, sliced very thin
1 head iceberg lettuce
1 green bell pepper, sliced thin

DRESSING

4 cloves garlic
1 teaspoon salt
¼ teaspoon black pepper

½ cup olive oil
¼ cup white vinegar
¼ cup fresh lime juice

1. Sauté the bacon in a large sauté pan until crispy. Remove the bacon, but keep it for later. Oh, and don't drain the fat from the pan. Because you'll need it. No really, we're not kidding.

2. Lightly salt and pepper the shrimp and sprinkle with cumin. Quickly sauté the shrimp in the bacon fat, turning constantly until pink and completely cooked.

3. Drain shrimp on paper towels. Place the shrimp in a bowl, cover, and refrigerate until well chilled.

4. Cut the tomatoes in wedges. Cut the onion in thin slices. Break up the lettuce by hand.

5. Toss all salad ingredients together with the sliced green pepper. Place all the vegetables in the refrigerator to chill.

6. Use a mortar and pestle to mash the garlic with the salt and pepper for the dressing.

7. Pour the olive oil, vinegar, and lime juice in a small bowl.

8. Add the crushed garlic and whisk together thoroughly. You can also use a blender to emulsify the oil and liquids.

9. Chop up the crispy cooked bacon into small sprinkle-size pieces.

10. Gradually add the dressing, a little at a time, while you toss the salad with a large salad fork. Add just enough dressing to cover the salad—more or less to your own taste.

11. Divide salad into individual serving bowls.

12. Place a generous serving of shrimp on each salad.

13. Generously sprinkle the salad as it glistens in the tropical sunshine with the crunchy bacon bits—wow, we're getting hungry just talking about this one.

Serves 6 to 8

Raúl: A nice salad is a good addition to any meal. A simple salad makes an appearance at just about every Cuban party.

Jorge: For a dinner party, we like to spruce up this simple salad with the great taste of bacon and some nice tender shrimp.

Glenn: There is something about parties and seafood, no matter where you live. A party is a great time to splurge a little, so it's no wonder you see so many people buying shrimp and lobster for their special events.

Ensalada de Frijoles Negros
Black Bean Salad

Jorge: Where would we be without the lowly black bean?

Jorge: Where would we be without the lowly black bean?

Raúl: Mothers in Cuba wean their kids on black beans and rice!

Glenn: I have to confess that I had never eaten a black bean before I came to Miami. Growing up in Minneapolis, the only bean dish we ever ate was Boston baked beans. I don't think anyone ever thought of making a Boston baked bean salad.

Jorge: This salad is easy to make and tastes great. You can even cheat and use canned black beans. We won't tell anybody if you won't.

1 pound dried black beans
9 cups water
1 tablespoon olive oil
1 cup diced green bell pepper, blanched
   (see step 4 below)

3 cups diced fresh tomato, seeded
½ cup chopped green onion
¼ cup chopped fresh cilantro

DRESSING

⅓ cup olive oil
⅓ cup fresh lime juice
3 tablespoons brown sugar

1½ teaspoons ground cumin
4 cloves garlic, peeled
Salt and black pepper to taste

1. Cover cleaned dry beans with water and let stand covered overnight. Discard water.

2. Place the black beans in a large 6-quart saucepan. Add water and olive oil—this will prevent the beans from foaming.

3. Bring the beans to a boil, reduce heat to low, cover, and cook until the beans are tender, about 1 hour.

NOTE: This is the part of the recipe, where you, at your option, can ignore the preceding instructions and slip in a couple cans of canned black beans, drained. Pay one of the neighborhood kids to create a precisely timed disturbance on your front lawn and none of those "back-seat cooks" (OK, we're thinking mother-in-law here) in your kitchen will be any the wiser . . .

4. Core and seed the green pepper. Blanch the pepper by dropping it into a pan of boiling, lightly salted water for just a minute or two.

5. Let the pepper cool and dice when cool enough to handle.

6. Combine the black beans, green pepper, tomatoes, green onion, and cilantro in a non-metallic bowl.

DRESSING

1. Use a blender to combine the olive oil, lime juice, brown sugar, cumin, and garlic.

2. Blend on high to grind up all the garlic.

(continued on page 211)

(continued from page 208)

3. Season the dressing with salt and freshly ground black pepper to taste.

4. Pour the dressing over the bean mixture, cover and refrigerate for 1 hour or more to let the flavors absorb into the beans.

5. Serve the salad chilled on a fresh lettuce leaf. This also makes a nice salsa-style side dish to serve with your favorite entrée.

If you do this right, your mother-in-law may actually compliment you on your mastery of bean cookery! (Test performed with a professional mother-in-law in a closed kitchen—your actual results may vary.)

Serves 4

Ensalada de Pescado y Piña
Fish and Pineapple Salad

Jorge: OK, we know what you're thinking: fish salad? You guys must be kidding!

Glenn: Yes, this creamy salad features tender pieces of cooked white fish with lettuce and the sweet taste of fresh pineapple.

Raúl: Not exactly the tuna salad you're used to getting at the local diner.

Glenn: This one didn't just escape from a can!

1 pound fresh white fish or tuna fillets
¼ cup white wine
¼ cup water
½ teaspoon salt
¼ cup chopped onion

¼ cup chopped celery
1½ cups fresh ripe pineapple chunks
1 cup sliced sweet red onion
1 head leaf lettuce (a nice Bibb lettuce works well too)

DRESSING
1 (8-ounce) package cream cheese, room temperature
2 tablespoons milk
2 tablespoons real mayonnaise
½ cup fresh ripe pineapple chunks

1 tablespoon sugar
2 teaspoons sweet Spanish paprika
2 teaspoons fresh lemon juice
Salt and pepper to taste

1. Poach the fish by placing the wine, water, salt, onion, and celery in a large covered sauté pan. There should be just enough water for the fish to swim in—not drown.

2. Bring the water to a boil, place the fish in the pan and cover; reduce heat to low and let simmer for about 8 to 10 minutes, or until the fish is just cooked through.

3. Remove the fish from the pan and break into bite-size pieces. Refrigerate.

   TIP: *Refrigerate and save this fish stock for use in another recipe.*

4. For the dressing, beat the cream cheese, milk, mayonnaise, and ⅓ cup fresh pineapple with an electric mixer until creamy. Add the sugar, paprika, and lemon juice. Salt and pepper to taste.

5. Toss the dressing with 1½ cups pineapple, onion, and lettuce. (Adjust the amount of lettuce to get the right consistency.)

6. Gently fold in the cooked fish. Cover and chill the salad in the refrigerator for a minimum of 1, but not more than 3 hours. That's just long enough for a good nap, and you look like you could use one about now.

7. Serve chilled.

Serves 6 to 8

Ensalada de Tomate
Tomato Salad

½ cup olive oil
1 cup diced red onion
4 cloves garlic, minced
⅓ cup lemon juice

Salt and black pepper to taste
1 green bell pepper, cut in bite-size pieces
4 large red ripe tomatoes, sliced thin

1. Heat the olive oil in a 2-quart saucepan until it is moderately hot—not deep-frying temperature, about 300 degrees F. If it starts to smoke, you have gone too far.

2. Toss in the onion, garlic, and lemon juice. Immediately remove the pan from the heat and stir constantly for a minute or two.

3. Let cool. Season to taste with salt and pepper. Refrigerate until ready to serve.

4. Blanch the green pepper by putting it into a glass bowl, cover, and microwave on high for 45 seconds.

5. Slice the tomatoes as thin as you can get them. Arrange the tomatoes and green peppers on a salad plate.

6. Just before serving, give the dressing a good whisking to blend the oil and lemon juice. Lightly drizzle the tomatoes and the green pepper with the dressing.

7. Serve chilled. (To make sure that everyone eats this, don't let anyone know that you have something decadently rich prepared for dessert. "What should I have, the healthy salad or the dessert?" Hmmm.)

Serves 4 (on holidays, this serves about 20 Cubans)

Glenn: I must confess that when I think of the holidays, I never think of salad.

Jorge: For most people, holidays are a time of indulgence, when you forget the diet or at least put it on hold.

Raúl: So who wants to fill up on salad?

Jorge: At a Cuban party, you know the food is good when no one touches the salad.

Glenn: However, we know people who insist on "eating healthy," even on the biggest holidays of the year.

Jorge: This simple salad fills the bill. It tastes so good, even the Three Guys will have a spoonful or two on their holiday plates.

Raúl: But we'll never let it crowd out the good stuff.

Ensalada Mixta
Mixed Green Salad

Jorge: Restaurants all over Havana have traditionally served various versions of this salad.

Raúl: It is a very traditional salad, and for lunch, it's almost a complete meal in itself.

Glenn: We say almost, because what meal is complete without dessert and a Cuban coffee?

Jorge: Many Cuban households use canned asparagus spears in this dish. If you really want to be authentic, go ahead and use the canned spears.

1 pound fresh tuna fillet
¼ cup white wine
¼ cup water
½ teaspoon salt
1 dozen asparagus spears
Fresh lemon juice
1 head Romaine lettuce

6 hard-boiled eggs, sliced
3 large red ripe tomatoes, sliced
½ medium red onion, sliced
1 (14-ounce) can artichoke hearts (not salad)
Black olives, pitted

DRESSING

4 cloves garlic
1 teaspoon salt
¼ teaspoon black pepper

½ cup olive oil
⅓ cup fresh lime juice

1. Poach the fish by placing the wine, water, and salt in a large covered sauté pan. Bring the water to a boil, place the fish in the pan and cover; reduce heat to low and let simmer for about 8 to 10 minutes, or until the fish is just cooked through.

2. Remove the fish from the pan and break into bite-size pieces. Refrigerate.

3. Lightly oil the asparagus spears and fry quickly on a grill or in a shallow frying pan. Add a squirt or two of fresh lemon juice. Ideally, the spears will blacken slightly. Neatly spaced grill marks are a nice touch. Remove spears from heat and chill.

4. For the dressing, use a mortar and pestle to mash the garlic with the salt and pepper. Pour the olive oil and lime juice in a small bowl.

5. Add the crushed garlic and whisk together thoroughly. You can also use a blender to emulsify the oil and liquids.

6. Clean and break apart the lettuce, arranging the lettuce leaves on a large serving plate or platter.

7. Artfully arrange the tuna, asparagus spears, hard-boiled eggs, tomatoes, red onion, artichoke hearts, and black olives on top of the lettuce. Drizzle the whole works with the dressing. Serve chilled.

Serves 4 to 6

VIKINGS AND CUBANS

You wouldn't think there would be any connection between Vikings and Cubans. (Except for the Swedish Viking in our group.) However, if you ever go fishing with a Cuban, you may be in for a surprise. Get a couple of Cubans in a canoe and you might be baffled—as Glenn was—to hear them shout, almost in unison, "Vikingos!"

"This happened just about every time Jorge and Raúl got into the canoe," Glenn reports. It seems there was a very popular television series in Cuba about the Viking explorers. Most of the show involved these intrepid Norsemen paddling from one conquest to another in their longboats. For Cubans this television show is long gone, but not forgotten.

Now, whenever the Three Guys get together for fishing, it's a tradition for someone to stand in the bow as we leave the dock and shout "Vikingos!" A sight, we're sure, that inspires shock and awe among any innocent bystanders.

Frijoles Negros
Black Beans and Rice

2½ cups dried black beans
9 cups water
1 tablespoon olive oil
1½ cups chopped onion
1½ cups chopped green bell pepper
3 cloves garlic, peeled, and mashed with
   1 teaspoon salt and ½ teaspoon black
   peppercorns

Olive oil for sautéing
1 teaspoon oregano
1 teaspoon ground cumin
1 bay leaf
3 tablespoons vinegar
¾ cup dry Spanish wine
2 teaspoons sugar
Olive oil

1. Cover dry beans with water and let stand covered overnight. Drain and discard water.

2. Place the cleaned black beans in a large 6-quart saucepan. Add water and olive oil—this will prevent the beans from foaming. Bring the beans to a boil, reduce heat to low, cover, and cook until the beans are tender, about 1 hour.

3. Do not add salt to the beans while they are cooking. Salt at this stage of the game will make your beans very tough.

4. You may also cook the beans in a pressure cooker. Follow the manufacturer's directions for exact times, but our pressure cooker takes about 20 to 25 minutes to cook the beans completely.

5. Whichever method you use, do not drain the water from the cooked beans.

6. Meanwhile, chop onion and green pepper. Mash the garlic with salt and peppercorns in a mortar and pestle.

7. Sauté the onions and green pepper in olive oil until the onions are translucent. Add mashed garlic and sauté another minute or so.

8. Add the cooked beans, oregano, cumin, bay leaf, vinegar, and wine. Cover and simmer over low heat for 15 to 20 minutes, stirring occasionally. Remove bay leaf.

9. Some cooks—including us—like to thicken the beans by taking about 1 cup of beans and mashing them to make a thick paste. Mix the mashed beans back into the pot.

10. Add additional salt and pepper to taste. Stir in the sugar; then drizzle a couple of tablespoons of olive oil over the beans. Immediately cover the pot, remove from heat, and let stand for 10 minutes.

11. Serve the by now fantastically prepared black beans over white rice.

You may garnish the beans with cilantro and chopped white onions. Not only do they look good presented this way, they taste even better than they look.

Jorge: There is one Cuban signature dish, a dish that Cubans eat at just about every meal, a side dish that no real Cuban ever gets tired of: frijoles negros, the black bean dish we worship and glorify.

Glenn: What does this mean for your intrepid cookbook authors? It means that we can't publish a Cuban party book without including this essential Cuban side dish.

Raúl: So if you've seen this recipe before, please bear with us and understand the necessity of bringing more converts into the Cuban Black Bean Brotherhood—and Sisterhood.

Serves 8

Fufú Dulce
Sweet Mashed Plantains

3 large, medium-ripe plantains
4 cups chicken stock or broth
¾ pound pork meat with fat
2 strips bacon, chopped
Olive oil for frying
½ cup chopped green onions

½ cup chopped white onion
4 cloves garlic, mashed
5 tablespoons butter, softened
2 tablespoons fresh lemon juice
¼ cup chopped cilantro leaves
Salt and pepper to taste

Jorge: Fufú is the Latin version of mashed potatoes.

Raúl: Many people prefer fufú that is starchy and not sweet. That's the most common version served in Miami restaurants.

Glenn: However, this recipe is closer to the Puerto Rican dish, mofongo. It calls for plantains that are no longer green and starting to ripen.

Raúl: In Miami, many restaurants mash the plantain at tableside in a dramatic presentation!

1. Cut the ends off the plantains and discard. Slice each plantain into 3-inch chunks and score the skin with a knife along one edge. Do not peel.

2. Place the plantains in a 3-quart saucepan, and add the stock. Bring to a boil, reduce heat to low, cover, and simmer until tender, about 20 to 30 minutes.

3. For meat, you need pork with plenty of fat—either well marbled or with a fat layer or both. We've had good luck using a Boston butt or pork shoulder roast.

4. Cut the meat into chunks—approximately 2½ inches square. Salt the meat by eye and place in a large 3-quart saucepan. Add water to just barely cover the meat.

5. Bring to a boil; reduce heat to low, and simmer, uncovered until all of the water has boiled away. There should be a small quantity of rendered liquid fat in the bottom of the pan. Add a little olive oil to the pan, more if your pork is a little on the lean side.

6. Fry the pork pieces and the bacon in the rendered fat just until brown, and slightly crispy. Don't be afraid to include some pieces of pork fat. The meat should be tender and stringy. Remove the meat and chop into small chunks.

7. Sauté the onions in the rendered fat at medium temperature, 3 to 5 minutes. Add the garlic and sauté a minute or two more. Return the meat to the pan.

8. Remove the fully cooked plantains from the broth (do not discard the broth) and remove the peels. (They should be falling off by now.)

9. Coarsley mash the plantains by hand with some of the broth, to the consistency of chunky mashed potatoes.

10. Mash in the butter. Add the mashed plantain, lemon juice, and cilantro to the fried pork, bacon, and onions, stirring constantly over low heat.

11. Salt and pepper to taste. Serve hot.

Serves 4

Papas con Tocino
Baked Potatoes with Bacon

Glenn: This is Raúl's favorite way to do potatoes on the grill. If you are making something on the grill, you can start your potatoes first while you get your meat or seafood ready.

Raúl: You can just as easily make these in the oven.

Jorge: The bacon gives the potatoes a nice smoky flavor and helps keep the skins moist.

Raúl: When the potatoes are done, cut them open and slightly smash with a fork.

Glenn: Add a little olive oil or butter and fresh chopped cilantro. Delicious.

6 to 8 large baking potatoes
6 to 8 strips hickory-smoked bacon
¼ cup olive oil or melted butter

2 tablespoons chopped cilantro
Salt and pepper to taste

1. Clean each potato thoroughly. Wrap each potato with a strip of bacon. Wrap in aluminum foil.

2. Place foil-wrapped potatoes on the grill and cook until fork tender, about 45 minutes to 1 hour. Turn potatoes occasionally to cook evenly.

   TIP: To add a smokier flavor, you can open the foil on the potatoes during the last 15 minutes of cooking.

   TIP: You can also cook these in a 375-degrees-F oven for about 1 hour.

3. Remove potatoes from foil, and remove bacon. Dice the bacon. Cut a cross into the top of each potato and push the ends together to open and break up the potato slightly.

4. Drizzle with olive oil or melted butter, and sprinkle with bacon bits and cilantro.

5. Salt and pepper to taste.

Serves 6 to 8

Cumpleaños—Cuban Birthday Parties

Glenn: Until the late 1950s, no Cuban birthday party was complete without an American-style birthday cake.

Jorge: Having a great cake was a status symbol. The best cakes came from bakeries. In many neighborhoods, a "cake lady" made delicious cakes in her home.

Glenn: Cuban birthday cakes are very elaborate with multiple layers, colorful frostings, and many decorations. A particularly Cuban touch? Plastic decorations that dot the top of the cake. Lucky kids find a small candy attached to the bottom of the decoration.

Raúl: At some parties, if you find a candy this way you win a small prize.

Jorge: One party game that is very Cuban is a game similar to leapfrog called "Pon." You have to hop over all of the kids in front of you until you get to the end of the line.

Glenn: Many people also organize treasure hunts for the children with clues written on slips of paper. The clues lead to small caches of hidden toys and candy.

Jorge: You might think that the piñata is strictly a Mexican tradition. However, in Cuba we had our own cardboard and colored-paper creations stuffed with candy and small prizes. Many people made piñatas in the shape of American cartoon characters—Mickey Mouse and Donald Duck were very popular. However, most of the home-made ones were less elaborate, like a cylinder made to look like a drum, or two round boxes made to resemble a cowboy hat.

Raúl: I went to a party once where the piñata was a huge white swan—it was enormous.

Glenn: There is no blindfold or baseball bat at a Cuban party. The Cuban piñata is built with a small trap door in the bottom. Ribbons are threaded through the trap door in such a way that one "magic ribbon" holds the trapdoor in place.

Jorge: All of the children gather around as the adults hoist the piñata above their heads. The mother of the birthday child counts to three and all of the children begin pulling on a ribbon—pink for girls and blue for boys. One lucky child pulls the magic ribbon, causing the trapdoor to open and all of the candy to fall on the floor.

Raúl: One nice thing about a Cuban piñata? Because you don't smash the piñata with a bat, you can use the same piñata over and over again.

Glenn: No child is left behind by an errant bat swing to the head either.

Papas y Fritas con Mayonesa
Potatoes with Mayonnaise

Jorge: I enjoyed this recipe when I was in Spain. Many restaurants and bars served this as a side dish or tapas dish.

Glenn: If Jorge enjoyed it, it has to be good, because he usually hates mayonnaise. He spent an entire school year forced to eat nothing but mayonnaise sandwiches every day in Cuba during the "special period."

Jorge: I only eat mayonnaise in this dish and in Imperial Rice.

Glenn: So if you are one of those people who hates mayonnaise, try this recipe anyway. You might really like it.

Raúl: Make sure you use a good quality vegetable oil heated to frying temperature. That will keep too much oil from soaking into the potatoes.

6 cups red or Yukon Gold potatoes, cut into ½-inch cubes
¼ cup water
⅓ cup mayonnaise
5 cloves garlic, minced
¼ cup parsley
Vegetable oil for frying
Salt and pepper to taste

1. Make sure you get potatoes with a thin skin. You can leave thin skins on; otherwise, you need to peel the potatoes, and who wants to do that if they don't have to?
2. Place the potato cubes in a small saucepan on the stove. Cover the potatoes with water in the pan, bring to a boil, reduce heat to low, cover and simmer for about 15 to 20 minutes.
3. Drain the potatoes thoroughly, but do not rinse. Use a paper towel to blot up any excess moisture.
4. Meanwhile, mix together by hand the mayonnaise, garlic, and parsley.
5. Heat vegetable oil (not olive oil!) about 3 inches deep in a large sauté pan to approximately 350 degrees F.
6. Fry the potato cubes in small batches in the hot oil until golden brown. Pre-cooking brings the starch out of the potatoes, so when you first drop them in the oil, stir carefully to prevent them from sticking together and watch out for any splatters.
7. Remove the potato cubes from the oil and drain thoroughly on paper towels. Keep hot.
8. Lightly toss the hot potatoes with the mayonnaise mixture. Salt and pepper to taste. Serve immediately.

Serves 4 to 6

Yuca con Salsa de Toronja y Naranja
Yuca with Grapefruit and Orange Sauce

2 pounds yuca peeled, quartered and cut
    into 2-inch chunks
6 cloves garlic, minced
Juice of 1 lime
¼ cup finely chopped cilantro leaves

½ cup olive oil
2 oranges, peeled and diced
1 grapefruit, peeled and diced
1 large sweet yellow onion, sliced thin
Salt and pepper to taste

1. Bring 6 quarts of salted water to a boil in a large stockpot. Add the cleaned and cut yuca to the pot, bring back to a boil, then reduce heat to low and simmer, uncovered, for about 40 to 50 minutes, or until the yuca is tender.

2. Set the yuca aside to cool, but don't drain it at this point.

3. Mix together the garlic, lime juice, and cilantro and add a little salt to taste.

4. Heat the olive oil in a small saucepan until it is hot, but not smoking, about 300 degrees F. Remove pan from heat. Pour the lime juice/garlic/cilantro mixture into the hot oil, whisking constantly for 1 or 2 minutes.

5. Add the oranges, grapefruit, and onion to the saucepan and let simmer over medium-low heat, stirring occasionally, until the onions have lost some of their crispness, about 5 to 10 minutes. Salt and pepper to taste.

6. Drain the yuca. Gently toss the yuca with the salsa.

Serves 6 to 8

Jorge: Yuca is a staple in most Cuban kitchens. One of the most popular recipes is for Yuca con Mojo, a delicious garlic-flavored sauce.

Raúl: We love it!

Glenn: This take on yuca features a delicious citrus salsa.

Jorge: The oranges and grapefruit give the yuca a whole new taste. It's a great change of pace!

THE VELORIO: EVERY CUBAN'S FINAL PARTY

A velorio is a Cuban wake. Traditionally held in the deceased's own home (though now just as likely to be held at a funeral home) the velorio features an open casket, so everyone gets one last look at the dearly departed.

Cuban wakes are by no means quiet affairs. There is a lot of loud talking and yes, even jokes and laughter at many wakes. A velorio is a time to get together with old friends and family members, drink café, and talk about everything from sports to politics. Many velorios include an elaborate variety of food.

In Cuba, the velorio normally lasted all night, with at least a person or two staying with the deceased until the funeral mass and burial the next day.

When one of the Three Guys from Miami goes, it will be up to the other two guys to throw him the best velorio ever!

Until that day, my friend, until that day . . .

Cuban FOOD GLOSSARY

Aquacate—an avocado. They are popular in salads or eaten plain, although there is no such thing as Cuban guacamole.

Arroz con Leche—rice pudding. This dessert is very sweet and creamy with a great taste of cinnamon. It sometimes includes raisins and is many times flavored with good Cuban rum.

Baño de Maria—the Spanish name for "water bath," a pan of water that goes in the oven. When making flan, you place the flan mixture into custard cups or a baking dish and then set these in the Baño de Maria. The water bath prevents the bottom of the flan from burning. We usually use a metal cake or jelly-roll pan with an inch or two of water as a Baño de Maria. However, you can use anything that holds water and can go in the oven.

Bijol—a powder made with annatto seeds. Cooks use Bijol instead of saffron for coloring rice in many recipes, mainly because saffron is expensive. Bijol does not really duplicate the saffron flavor; however, it does have a unique flavor all its own that is unmistakable in Cuban dishes. You may substitute ground annatto or achiote seeds, usually found in Latin and Mexican markets. Some Cuban cooks use achiote oil to color rice, although purists claim that the oil has a different flavor than Bijol or ground annatto.

Boniato—a Cuban sweet potato that is drier than and not as sweet as the common American varieties. In flavor, it is a cross between a sweet and a baking potato, with a fluffier texture and a very mild taste.

Calabaza—a type of pumpkin used in cooking. Its flavor is closer to squash than to pumpkin. Just about every Latin and Mexican market stocks calabaza in season. If it's not available in your area, you may substitute butternut squash for calabaza in most recipes.

Chorizo—a type of sausage. Cuban cooking uses a Spanish variety that is not hot and spicy like its Mexican cousin. Spanish chorizo is a dry, hard sausage heavily flavored with garlic and paprika. A good chorizo is the essential building block of an excellent paella.

Cilantro and Culantro—two plants that look different but taste a lot alike. Cilantro has a sharper bite than its cousin does. Culantro has a somewhat musty flavor. Cooks use both herbs in Cuba. In fact, culantro grew wild all over the island. Many Cuban cooks prefer to use culantro for its subtly different flavor.

Congri—Please don't confuse this dish, as many do, with Moros y Cristianos. The dishes are similar in that you cook the beans with the rice. However, you make the traditional Congri of Cuba Oriente with red beans instead of black.

Croquetas—a filling of meat or fish with a light batter. You deep-fry these delicious little snacks until golden brown. On the appetizer menu in many restaurants, they are a favorite walk-away item at bakeries and coffee windows.

Empanadas—fluffy turnovers filled with ham, beef, picadillo, cheese, or other ingredients.

Flan—a rich egg custard. Flan is poured into a pan with a coating of dark caramelized sugar. Once baked in the oven, the caramel liquefies to create a delicious thin syrup.

Frijoles Negros—black beans in a thick gravy of garlic, onion, green pepper, and spices. It's the signature dish of Cuba, eaten at just about every meal, and is usually served over rice as a side dish.

Frituras—what Americans would call fritters. You make Cuban frituras from dough that may include several root vegetables, such as malanga or boniato. They also may contain fish or meat with onions, garlic, peppers, and other spices.

Fufú or Fufú de Plátanos Verdes—a dish similar to mashed potatoes. Fufú has a delicious garlic flavor with a hint of lemon or lime. What really makes it sing are the tasty pieces of roast pork mashed into the plantain.

Guayaba—guava, used as a filling in cakes and pastries.

Maduros, or Plátanos Maduros—sweet plantain, sliced diagonally and sautéed. Plantains need to be very ripe, almost black before cooking. They are very sweet with a strong banana-and-caramelized-sugar flavor.

Malanga—another root vegetable that is popular with Cubans. It comes in both white and yellow varieties. Malanga is very closely related to the taro root. It is very digestible and many mothers use it as a baby food. Malanga is also often made into flour and used in cakes, breads, and pastries. Malanga flour is a great substitute for cornstarch to thicken or "tighten up" stews and sauces, and malanga fritters are also very popular. Most Latin and Mexican groceries sell malanga.

Mariscos—seafood, so arroz con mariscos is simply "seafood with rice." Mariscos usually include shrimp, scallops, lobster, fish, clams, mussels, and so on.

Masa Flour (Masa Harina)—a corn flour used to make tamales. It's also used as a thickening agent in many dishes.

Mojo (Mojito)—used as a marinade and sauce. You can make it very simply with sour orange juice, loads of garlic, onions, and spices.

Moros y Cristianos—similar to frijoles negros, but you cook the beans together with the rice.

Parboiled Rice—made by soaking, steaming, and drying rice before it goes through the milling process. The most popular parboiled rice in the United States is Uncle Ben's Converted Rice. Many Latin food companies sell their own brand of parboiled rice. For years, chefs looked down their collective noses at parboiled rice, but in recent years, even gourmet chefs have developed an appreciation for this rice, because it cooks up fluffy and separate. Contrary to popular belief, the parboiling process actually drives the nutrients into the rice grain, making parboiled rice more nutritious than standard white rice.

Picadillo—Cuban-style hash (some call it the Cuban Sloppy Joe) and a favorite meal of most Cubans. It's ground beef with tomato, green pepper, green olives, or capers and, of course, plenty of garlic. It's frequently served over rice with tostones on the side.

Saffron Strands—the cheaper alternative to pure saffron, which is one of the world's most expensive spices. You can usually find these at any Latin market or in the spice section of your local supermarket. Many people dry the strands in a warm oven. You may also crush them right out of the package with a mortar and pestle. To avoid any saffron "grit" in your dish, you can also steep saffron strands in a little warm water to make saffron "tea." Run the tea through a strainer and you have essential saffron flavoring.

Stock/Broth—whether chicken, beef, or ham. Avoid using meat-flavored bouillon cubes (Caldo Concentrado) in any recipe. They consist mostly of salt. It's always best to make your own stock. You can simmer beef bones and trimmings, chicken bones and skin, a hambone, and so on, in water to make a delicious and natural stock. Canned broths will do in a pinch. There are also a couple of brands of stock that you can keep in the refrigerator. These products are sold as wet pastes, not dry granules. The key is to look at the label. The first ingredient listed should be meat, chicken, beef, or ham depending on the stock. Brands we like include Tone's for chicken and beef stock (sold at Sam's Clubs among others), and Redi-Base for ham stock. Just add the stock concentrate to hot water and you have a delicious stock for use in recipes.

Tamales—the ones we make are not very much like the Mexican version. Cuban tamales are not spicy hot, and the meat is mixed in with the dough. If you order just one, it's called a tamal—never a tamale. "Tamales" is the plural form of tamal. That's why Glenn avoids any confusion and always asks for two.

Tasajo—dried beef that's been reconstituted. You can use it in a stew with tomatoes and spices, or serve it fried. A real traditional Cuban comfort food.

Tortilla—a Cuban egg dish similar to an omelet or frittata; it usually includes potatoes and onions. However, there are many variations, including some with ham, cheese, chorizo, rice, shrimp, and even ripe plantain.

Tostones—thick slices of plantain, fried, flattened, and fried again, then salted and served hot.

Turrones—almond candies imported from Spain and are a traditional holiday treat. They come in several flavors, including chocolate, nougat, honey, fruit, and egg.

Yuca—another one of the root vegetables that are staples in Cuba. The most common preparation is with lemon, garlic, and olive oil—a great side dish. Most Americans have eaten yuca without even knowing it. Have you ever had tapioca? All tapioca products come from yuca. Yuca flour is also used in cooking, especially as a thickening agent.

Sources

It used to be that you could only find Latin ingredients in specialty markets in the larger cities. Wow, how times have changed! With more interest in Cuban and Latin cooking you can now find many ingredients at your local grocery store. There has also been an explosion of Latin and ethnic markets in cities and towns all over America. These small stores often carry many ingredients that are essential in a Cuban kitchen: fruits like mangos, guava, and papaya; root vegetables like yuca, *malanga,* and *boniato;* and of course, the ubiquitous plantain.

If you can't find an ingredient in your area, check out one of these Latin food sources:

AMIGOFOODS

AmigoFoods.com is a great Internet source for all types of Latin foods: Cuban, Argentinean, Brazilian, Chilean, Colombian, Dominican, Mexican, Peruvian, Puerto Rican, Spanish, Uruguayan, and Venezuelan. They carry some hard to find items like Bijol, sour orange juice (in bottles), and tasajo, even canned yuca—sounds bad, but actually tastes pretty good.

AmigoFoods.com
7501 NE 3rd Place
Miami, FL 33138
1.800.627.2544

TIENDA.COM FINE PRODUCTS FROM SPAIN

Internet-based Tienda.com is a great source for Spanish chorizo, morcilla, serrano ham, cheeses, olive oil, smoked paprika (pimentón), spices, sidra, and a nice selection of Spanish wines.

Tienda.com
3701 Rochambeau Road
Williamsburg, VA 23188
757.566.9606
888.472.1022 toll free
757.566.9603 fax
www.tienda.com

CUBAN FOOD MARKET

Everything for the Cuban chef. If you can't find it here, it's probably not available on the Internet. Items include a full range of spices, guava pastes and jellies, sour orange juice *(naranja agria),* prepared mojo marinades, beans, fruits, and vegetables. It's the only place online that we know of where you can get real *cachucha* peppers.

Cuban Food Market
3100 SW 8 Street
Miami, FL 33135
877.999.9945 toll free
305.644.8861 fax
www.cubanfoodmarket.com

Acknowledgments

Special thanks to our sister and sister-in-law Norma. She claims she doesn't know how to cook, but her tips and advice have been invaluable.

Thanks also to Nephew Neil who is a tireless promoter of our efforts and who has been the catalyst for many good times and great parties.

All the abuelas of the world for their opinions and comments.

Diane Moore who never stops talking about us, or anything else for that matter.

The people of Miami for their support and encouragement.

Marty Snortum, a Texan, and a **vegan** at that, who creates such lovingly composed portraits of foods he can never eat.

Harriet Granthen who proves that food styling is an art, she has elevated our dishes to new heights.

Melissa Barlow, our editor at Gibbs Smith. She has an eagle eye, a great sense of humor, and is second to only the Great Salt Lake as a reason to visit Utah.

Eliott Rodriguez, Alison Einerson, Wily Chirino, Lynne Rossetto Kasper, Mark DeCarlo, Alina Valle, Oscar Lopez, David Mullins, Robert and Lisa Zarranz, Sarah Brueggemann, everyone at "Despierta América," and Eric Perkins for helping us promote our first book, *Three Guys From Miami Cook Cuban.*

About the
THREE GUYS FROM MIAMI

Glenn Lindgren, Raúl Musibay, and Jorge Castillo are the Three Guys from Miami. They run the website iCuban.com: the Internet Cuban and are the authors of *Three Guys from Miami Cook Cuban* (Gibbs Smith, Publisher). Their website debuted in 1996 and since then more than 5 million people have visited the Three Guys online.

For more than twenty years, the Three Guys From Miami have been perfecting their Cuban recipes by cooking and eating—oh yes, a lot of eating—Cuban food. They have made several appearances on national TV. They are frequent sources of Cuban cooking tips and advice for both professional and amateur chefs all over the world.

GLENN LINDGREN

Glenn grew up in Minneapolis and first came to Miami in 1984. Here he fell in love with the tropical city with its friendly people and unique Cuban culture. Glenn leads a double life: most of the year he poses as a regular Swedish guy from Minnesota. His neighbors and even many of his friends and family members don't know that every time he steps off the plane in Miami, he becomes an honorary Cuban and one of the Three Guys From Miami. When not in the kitchen, Glenn documents the antics of the Three Guys in books, magazines, and on the Internet. Although he spends a lot of quality time in Miami, (usually in the winter) Glenn and his wife Maureen live in Eagan, Minnesota, with two daughters, Erin and Gabrielle, and a son, Dennis.

RAÚL MUSIBAY

A native Cuban, Raúl came to the United States via Spain in 1980. As a full-time Miami resident, Raúl is known for his love of fishing, his great parties, and his mastery of the Cuban pig roast. Like Hemingway's *Old Man and the Sea*, Raúl frequently braves the ocean waves in the Florida Keys with his small fishing boat. Just don't call him old. He insists that he gets a little better, but never older, every year. A somewhat reluctant chef, Raúl is the goodwill ambassador of the group. You'll find him at cooking classes and demonstrations "working the crowd," telling jokes, and making sure everyone is having a good time. Raúl and his wife Esther have two married children, Onel and Onix. Raúl's mother, Amparo, and mother-in-law, Georgina, make up the rest of his extended family.

JORGE CASTILLO

Jorge came to the United States via the Mariel Boatlift in 1980. Although born and raised in Cayo la Rosa, Jorge left Miami after three months to live in Iowa, where he mastered the English language and learned to love corn on the cob, root beer, and Cookie's Barbecue Sauce. In Iowa, he also met his future wife Mary and set in motion a series of fortunate events that would eventually result in the creation on the Three Guys From Miami. Jorge is the artist of the group, at least when it comes to food. Unlike his two brothers-in-law, he has always had an eye for artistic food presentation. Jorge has lived for the past eight years in the West Kendall area of Miami with Mary and their two daughters, Mariel and Allison.

Index

Raúl: Hey man, what's going on?

Jorge: Yeah, why are we stopping?

Glenn: Well guys, we just finished writing our second cookbook.

Raúl: We have? Wow, I didn't even know we were writing one!

Jorge: Are you sure that's it?

Glenn: Yes, this is it. The last page in the book.

Raúl: You know what?

Glenn: Hmm?

Raúl: This calls for a celebration!

Jorge: Did someone say party?